The High-Conflict Couple

Dialectical Behavior Therapy
Guide to Finding Peace,
Intimacy & Validation

Alan E. Fruzzetti, Ph.D.

EasyRead Large

Copyright Page from the Original Book

Publisher's Note

This publication is designed to provide accurate and authoritative information in regard to the subject matter covered. It is sold with the understanding that the publisher is not engaged in rendering psychological, financial, legal, or other professional services. If expert assistance or counseling is needed, the services of a competent professional should be sought.

Distributed in Canada by Raincoast Books

Copyright © 2006 by Alan E. Fruzzetti
New Harbinger Publications, Inc.
5674 Shattuck Avenue
Oakland, CA 94609
www.newharbinger.com

Cover design by Amy Shoup; Acquired by Catharine Sutker; Text design by Tracy Marie Carlson; Edited by Brady Kahn

All Rights Reserved
Printed in the United States of America

Library of Congress Cataloging-in-Publication Data

Fruzzetti, Alan E.
 The high-conflict couple : a dialectical behavior therapy guide to finding peace, intimacy, and validation / Alan E. Fruzzetti.
  p. cm.
 ISBN-13: 978-1-57224-450-4
 ISBN-10: 1-57224-450-X
 1. Interpersonal conflict. 2. Marital conflict. 3. Emotions. 4. Dialectical behavior therapy. I. Title.
BF637.I48F78 2006
158.2—dc22

2006028315

08   07   06

10   9   8   7   6   5   4   3   2   1

First printing

TABLE OF CONTENTS

Foreword	v
Acknowledgments	ix
Chapter 1: Understanding Emotion in Relationships	1
Chapter 2: Accepting Yourself and Your Partner	31
Chapter 3: How to Stop Making Things Worse	61
Chapter 4: Being "Together" When You Are Together	81
Chapter 5: Reactivating Your Relationship	114
Chapter 6: Accurate Expression	146
Chapter 7: Validating Responses: What to Validate and Why	192
Chapter 8: Validating Responses: How to Validate Your Partner	222
Chapter 9: Recovering from Invalidation	262
Chapter 10: Managing Problems and Negotiating Solutions	296
Chapter 11: Transforming Conflict into Closeness	328
References	363

This is a long awaited book! Fruzzetti is a master clinician who does rigorous science in order to provide those of us doing treatment and those in need of it something that works. This is hope for all of us working with individuals, couples and families who suffer. Thank you, Alan, for this timely and important work.
—Suzanne Witterholt, MD, distinguished fellow of the American Psychiatric Association and director of Ananda Services for Dialectical Behavior Therapy in the Department of Psychiatry at the University of Minnesota

Fruzzetti is a leader in work with high-conflict couples and families. This muchawaited book provides an opportunity to learn his techniques and strategies, presented in his unique teaching style that is so effective. The book is a must for every DBT program as well as all those working within the field.
—Perry D. Hoffman, Ph.D., president of the National Education Alliance for Borderline Personality Disorder, New York

The High Conflict Couple performs a major public service. Fruzzetti's approach starts with an important principle: that dysregulated emotions are the core difficulty for high-conflict couples. From this he provides step-by-step practical methods designed to enhance acceptance, intimacy, and communication based on the latest research regarding emotion regulation and his own vast experience in working with couples and families. In essence, this is an excellent book, useful for both clinicians and couples regardless of the severity of their difficulties.
—Thomas R. Lynch, Ph.D., associate professor in the Departments of Psychiatry and Psychology and Neuroscience and director of the Cognitive Behavior Research and Treatment Program at Duke University

A warm and professional guide following in the tradition of acceptance and compassion. A book on how to handle love and stay connected even in difficult circumstances. We have waited for it!

—Anna Kåver, psychologist and author with Karolinska Hospital, Stockholm, Sweden

For my mentors, Dr. Marsha M. Linehan and the late Dr. Neil S. Jacobson

Foreword

Marsha M. Linehan, Ph.D.

No relationship has only smooth sailing. All relationships have conflict and an excess of negative emotion, so problems in intimate relationships affect just about everyone at one time or another. Being in a high-conflict relationship is exhausting and leaves both partners feeling miserable and alone. Being in an unhappy and distressed partnership is associated with increased rates of depression, anxiety, and substance use. Children in homes with great conflict are more likely to be troubled and even suicidal. This book addresses how to improve our intimate relationships, and in turn, our own and our family's well-being.

The book is based on the principles of dialectical behavior therapy (DBT), a treatment that has a large number of clinical trials demonstrating its effectiveness. DBT was developed at the University of Washington and Alan Fruzzetti was part of the very first DBT treatment team. He and the other members of the team gave the first critical feedback on the treatment and were major contributors to the development of the treatment in its current form. Alan has been working with DBT for twenty years, teaching it and adapting it for couples, families, and adolescents. Almost all of the research to date has focused on applying DBT to individuals, with few studies including families. Thus, there is a real absence in the literature: how to apply DBT to couples and families.

Dr. Fruzzetti is an expert in couple and family therapy and in research on intimate relationships. He is at the fore of work in this area, integrating mindfulness, emotion regulation, accurate expression, and validation into a coherent package. He has written dozens of professional articles and book chapters, both about DBT and about couple and family interactions and treatments from a DBT perspective.

In this book, Alan takes his expertise in working with couples and integrates it with his expertise in DBT. Like DBT, the book takes a nonjudgmental approach that promotes both acceptance of yourself and your partner, such as being mindful of yourself and your partner, and being more self-validating. It also focuses on change, such as reducing invalidation and negative responses to yourself and your partner while increasing your own emotion self-regulation, improving your ability to express yourself accurately, and building your skills to manage problems more effectively. The book also focuses heavily on the integration of these two strategies (acceptance and change), really helping you and your partner to be more validating toward each other.

It is very important to note that this book is based on sound principles and research, including research on basic emotional processes, couple interaction research, and the many studies evaluating dialectical behavior therapy. Very few books like this are actually based on research, so that puts this book into a very elite group.

The approach in this book is sensitive to the needs of struggling spouses and partners who have a lot of hurts and hopes. It addresses a broad variety of situations that couples find themselves in and provides thoughtful and practical ideas and practice exercises to help people decrease destructive conflict and find more peace and intimacy in their relationships.

Acknowledgments

Most people are lucky to have one real mentor in their lives. I have been very fortunate to have had several. Relevant to this book, in particular, is the inspiration I have received from my mentor, friend, and colleague Marsha Linehan, whose development of dialectical behavior therapy (DBT) is one of the truly innovative achievements in psychotherapy in the past couple of decades. In addition, my former research advisor and mentor Neil Jacobson, who died much too young in 1999, taught me a great deal about couples therapy, couple interaction, and about research, and inspired me to try new ideas and approaches to complex problems. These are two people whose shoes I cannot hope to fill.

My friend and colleague Perry Hoffman has for years provided support and friendship and has collaborated with me to adapt DBT to work with families. Her tirelessness for alleviating suffering in families continues to guide me. Many other colleagues and friends have contributed to my thinking about DBT and how to apply DBT to the problems of couples and families, provided feedback about the ideas in this book, given feedback about related papers or earlier drafts of the chapters in this book, and/or provided helpful and ongoing encouragement. These include, in particular, Linda Dimeff, Christine Foertsch, Anna Kåver, Beverly Long, Elizabeth Malmquist, Richelle Moen-Moore, Alec Miller, Åsa Nilsonne, Anita Olsson, Joan Russo, Renee Schneider, Doug Snyder, Liz Simpson, Charlie Swenson, and Suzanne Witterholt.

Over the past many years I have been lucky to have wonderful therapists in our DBT Couple and Family Clinic. Many have participated in the development of the ideas in this book and helped pilot and/or evaluate parts of this work. Special appreciation goes to Jill Compton, Kate Iverson, Liz Mosco, Becky Pasillas, Jennifer Sayrs, Chad Shenk, and Steven Thorp.

Of course, most of what we learn about couples comes from them. So, I want to extend a special thank you to the many couples who have participated in various research projects studying basic couple interaction processes or evaluating the impact of various interventions. In addition, many people involved in Family Connections programs, both leaders and participants, have given me ideas, inspiration, and support.

And, Thich Nhât Hanh's extensive work on mindfulness and on using understanding to alleviate suffering has guided much of my work.

Much credit and appreciation also go to the people at New Harbinger Publications, in particular Matt McKay and Catharine Sutker, for their commitment to this book and for their ongoing support of its ideas, and to Brady Kahn, for her thoughtful and very helpful editing. They have been such a pleasure to have as colleagues.

My family has provided everything I needed to do this work. I am grateful to my wonderful children for being who they are. And my wife, *mi esposa maravillosa* Armida, continues to provide the love, passion, intellect, and emotional partnership that make my life the rich and rewarding adventure that it is. Without her love and support, I never could have started, much less finished, this book.

Chapter 1

Understanding Emotion in Relationships

Why is it we sometimes say the nastiest things to the person we love the most? How is it that seemingly simple negotiations sometimes end up with partners screaming at each other? How do we end up snapping and acting in ways we swore we would never do again? What makes people who love each other sometimes get really anxious when approaching each other, or leads us to avoid talking about important matters? And, more importantly, how can we learn to stop long-standing patterns of destructive conflict, develop the skills to manage our negative emotions and destructive urges, and learn how to talk and listen in ways that lead to understanding, validation, negotiation, and closeness? These are the questions this book will address.

Everyone knows, minutes or hours after a nasty fight, that what we said made things worse and got us less of what we wanted. Yet, somehow we said it or did it anyway and may even have meant it at the moment. But now, with emotional arousal back to normal, guilt, remorse, regret, hurt, and grief set in. Maybe we will be able to apologize and turn things around, but the whole episode is likely to happen again and again. Destructive conflict in couples corrodes relationships and makes both partners miserable. The central idea in this book is that highly aroused, negative emotion—*dysregulated emotion*—is the core problem for highconflict couples and that there are specific skills partners can learn to manage their emotions effectively, which in turn makes effective communication (accurate expression followed by understanding and validation) possible. With enough practice, conflict can be transformed into closeness and couples can achieve the closeness, friendship, intimacy, peace, and support that brings us joy and reduces our suffering.

Understanding Emotions and High Emotional Arousal

Emotions are much more complicated than most people realize. Part of the problem stems from the way we talk about emotion. First of all, we talk about emotion as a thing (a noun), rather than as something we are doing. But, in fact, emotions are complex processes like walking or talking, things that we actually *do* that affect other things inside us and also affect others. It is easier to conceptualize thinking as something that we do. Then, when we say we had a thought, we recognize that it was just one moment, one small piece, of a long process. Emotion can be conceptualized the same way. Thus, an emotion is just one moment out of a long process of emoting or feeling. Unfortunately, we don't have a good word for the process or for the whole system in which we have emotions.

How Emotions Work

There are many components to our emotion system. At any given moment, there are events going on all around us, such as sights and sounds and other aspects of the physical and social world. There are also events going on inside us, such as memories, images, thoughts, or sensations. All of these events, in addition to our attention, and our sensation and perception systems (which allow us to be aware of what's going on), influence emotion directly. With new developments in neuroscience almost daily, it's clear that there are many biological and biochemical processes in our brains that influence the course of emotions. However, the extent to which we are aware of our emotions, how we label them (and whether we are accurate), and how we express them also profoundly affect the process. And, finally, how others respond to us—particularly people we are close to—shapes the direction of our emotion in very important ways. Certain responses, such as understanding and validating our experience, soothe our frayed emotional edges, but others, such as criticizing or invalidating our experience, are like salt in an open wound in our hearts.

Emotion Dysregulation and Out-of-Control Behavior

Emotional arousal affects other systems directly, such as thinking and physical action. Thus, when we regulate or manage our emotion, we also are regulating our ability to think and act in ways that are effective and move us forward in our relationships, at work, or with other activities in life. It's been known for almost one hundred years that small to moderate amounts of stress and arousal keep people alert and interested, actually increasing self-control and performance on just about any kind of task (Yerkes and Dodson 1908). It's also true that past a moderate point of stress and arousal, self-control and performance begin to drop (Mandler 1993). At high enough levels of arousal, we begin to focus very narrowly on simply escaping from the aversive state of high negative emotion. This process can take a long time to build up or may happen instantly.

Regardless, once our orientation is on escape, we can consider ourselves *out of control.* Notice that this is not a pejorative label. Rather, being out of control describes a natural state in which we are not thinking or acting in a very clear way; we are no longer focused on our longer-term goals but are increasingly focused on the immediate goal of reducing this negative tension or arousal. The point at which we reorient our attention to escape may be considered the point at which emotion dysregulation begins; when our emotion system becomes dysregulated, it interferes with optimal cognitive and other self-control functions (Fruzzetti et al. 2003).

Thus, being dysregulated is not the same as being upset. You can be upset and still be quite able to make effective decisions, hold your tongue, or otherwise "control" yourself—manage to act in ways that help you achieve a better relationship, a better life, rather than simply escaping an unpleasant (or even awful) situation by doing something that hurts the other person, escalates the conflict, or, in general, makes things worse in the long run.

In reality, this kind of dysregulated or out-of-control behavior occurs rather frequently, on a continuum from very destructive out-ofcontrol behaviors, such as substance use or aggression, to less destructive ones, such as saying mean things or avoiding difficult situations. For example, when one partner is nagging at the other, being critical, the other's arousal goes up. It becomes difficult to remember that the complainer is somebody you love, and who loves you back. Sometimes it might only take a second; at other times you might feel it coming well in advance, but eventually you lose your balanced perspective and say something mean or nasty in return. The point here is not that it's unreasonable or unfair to respond to criticism with criticism—it might be fair—but rather that it just makes things worse for both people individually and for the relationship. Individual and relationship well-being would be improved if each partner were able to respond differently.

At this point, you might be thinking, "So, are you saying I'm just supposed to be a doormat and accept being treated badly?" That's a good question, and the answer is no, because there is a third or middle path between being resigned to being treated badly, on the one hand, and both people treating each other badly, on the other hand. The alternative is to break the cycle, responding in a way that deescalates the conflict without reducing self-respect. In order to do that, you must first understand how you get into these hair-trigger situations that lead you to create negative interactions or respond badly to your partner when he or she is already behaving badly.

Vulnerability to Negative Emotional Experiences

There are several factors that make you vulnerable to high negative emotional arousal and subsequent emotion dysregulation. They include how *sensitive* you are to relationship events and things your partner (or others) says or does; *reactivity,* or how much you react when you do perceive stressful or negative events; and *time to equilibrium,* or how long it takes you to return to "normal" emotionally (Linehan 1993a; Fruzzetti and Iverson 2006; Fruzzetti, Shenk, and Hoffman 2005).

Sensitivity

Some people are more emotionally sensitive than others, just as some people have more sensitive hearing, more sensitive taste, and so on. People with greater emotional sensitivity can sometimes tell what those with less sensitivity are feeling before they know it themselves. This can be unsettling in a conversation if not handled properly. People with high emotional sensitivity seem to grasp intuitively how other people are feeling, coping, and so on. Conversely, a person with low emotional sensitivity can sometimes have a really hard time intuitively understanding what another person is feeling. This person may need to have a lot more explaining and more direct and specific requests in order to be emotionally supportive and responsive. Low emotional sensitivity can leave a spouse or partner feeling misunderstood or even lead to falsely (but understandably) believing that the other person doesn't care about him or her.

To make matters more complicated, people can be sensitive about some topics or situations but not about others. These differences in overall emotional sensitivity result from ordinary developmental processes, the way conflict situations were handled by parents during childhood, as well as from the basic temperament with which you were born. But more specific sensitivities can develop in any relationship. Many couples have theme fights or topics about which one or both partners tend to be sensitive. Similarly, one partner may have high sensitivity left over from a previous relationship or from the current relationship about things that happened even years ago. Understanding each other's sensitivities can help couples learn how to communicate more effectively, and trying to increase or decrease your own sensitivity can also promote more effective interactions. Chapters 2, 3, and 7 cover this topic in greater depth.

Reactivity

Regardless of how sensitive any of us may be, when we do notice something that is emotionally relevant, our reaction may be small or large. Big reactions are often louder, more rapidly and intensely expressed, and are accompanied by higher emotional arousal. Thus, big reactions (high reactivity) can communicate more clearly what a person is feeling, but also can result in the person sometimes reacting too quickly, getting upset or even dysregulated before all the information has become available. This can sometimes be counterproductive, of course: if reactivity had been lower, the person's response might have been quite different and more productive. Conversely, small reactions—often quieter, slower, and less intensely expressed—allow time to understand the whole picture but may not effectively communicate how important something is or what someone is feeling, easily resulting in misunderstanding. Learning to regulate reactivity (more intense and rapid expression or less intense and rapid expression) is an important part in learning to manage our own emotions, which this book will focus on.

Time to Reach Equilibrium

Everyone has a kind of emotional equilibrium, or baseline level of emotional arousal. By definition, emotional equilibrium is a regulated state, in which we can think and act clearly, purposefully, and effectively. When our arousal goes up, it takes a certain amount of time to come back down to baseline. For some people, this happens very quickly, perhaps in only seconds or a few minutes. For others, it may take many minutes or even several hours. Not only is it painful to have negative emotional arousal be high for a long time, it also means that during this time, individuals are vulnerable to both increased reactivity and to becoming dysregulated, because their arousal is already elevated. Understanding how long it takes to return to emotional equilibrium can help couples decide whether, when, and for how long they should take a break when discussing particularly emotional topics.

Putting the pieces together, you can see that high emotion sensitivity, high reactivity, and slow return to equilibrium make you vulnerable to getting upset, or dysregulated, in a variety of situations, as is shown in figure 1. Before even considering the specifics of a given situation or what your partner is doing, you already may be on the path toward a destructive reaction.

How High Emotional Arousal Affects Your Relationship

There are many ways that negative emotional arousal affects your relationship, both directly and indirectly. For example, it may lead you to overreact in some situations, and perhaps even to underreact in others. This, in turn, makes it more difficult for your partner to respond in understanding, soothing, or loving ways: he or she simply doesn't have accurate information on which to base a response. So, even if your partner wants to respond in a loving way, and doesn't have his or her own negative emotional arousal to deal with (which is unlikely), it makes the job harder. (Figure 1)

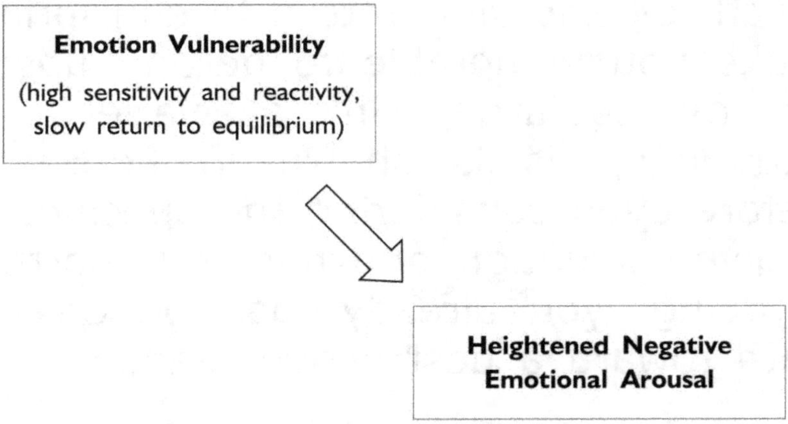

Emotion Vulnerability
(high sensitivity and reactivity, slow return to equilibrium)

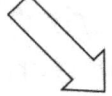

Heightened Negative Emotional Arousal

Figure 1

High Arousal Leads to Inaccurate Expression

As discussed earlier, when our emotional arousal is very high, our ability to take a balanced or long-term view suffers, and our thinking and reasoning abilities are similarly overwhelmed. Consequently, we say and do things that reflect being overwhelmed, we become defensive, or we simply do not describe the heartfelt desires and emotions that lie beneath our negative arousal. Figure 2 shows how this may unfold: high emotion vulnerability means that before anything much even happens, just as you enter the situation, your arousal shoots up, because, first, you are emotionally sensitive, either in general or in this kind of situation; second, you are reactive (again, perhaps in general, or only in this kind of situation); and third, you are slow to return to emotional equilibrium. Once your arousal goes up, your thinking abilities go down, and you start to lose the emotional balance that is needed to communicate effectively. Your high arousal also fuels negative and judgmental thinking, which further fuels negative emotional arousal—a vicious cycle. Then, being upset and having a lot of negative and judgmental thinking, you say things that don't reflect what you really want (closeness, attention, understanding), but instead say something bitter or nasty (inaccurate expression). This, of course, creates hurt feelings in your partner, furthers misunderstanding, and incites conflict.

For example, you might want to spend more time with your mate and be disappointed that he or she will be coming home late today. But, your negative arousal is the only thing you notice; you pay attention to that and have urges to escape from the situation, either by withdrawing or by pushing the other away emotionally. You become judgmental ("what a jerk"), which jacks up your emotion further. Then, instead of accurately expressing your disappointment, and also saying that you're longing for more closeness and time together (accurate expression), you criticize your partner for being selfish or just roll your eyes and show dismay or even contempt. (Figure 2)

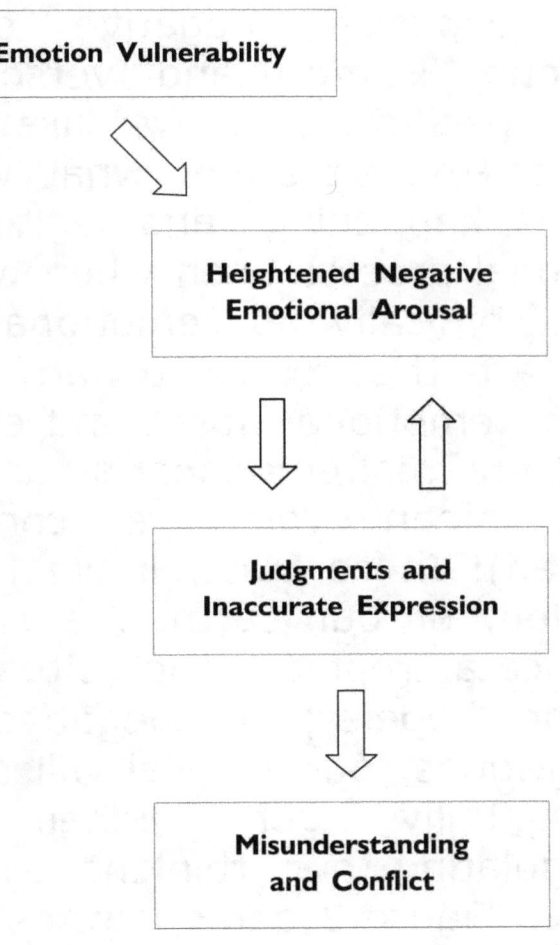

Figure 2

Inaccurate Expression Also Increases Arousal

It turns out that the way we think about the situation and what we tell ourselves about it can either soothe our emotions or act as a catalyst for even more explosive negative emotional reactions (Fruzzetti and Iverson 2006). More specifically, if we are able to describe the situation, what we want, what is happening, and legitimize the emotional process even when we do not like it, typically our emotional arousal will start the return toward a lower state of emotional upset and eventually back to normal emotional arousal (which might mean you are content or satisfied). In contrast, if we judge the situation, or our partner, as wrong or bad, catastrophize the situation, or become hopeless or negative in our expectations, our arousal will stay high or actually get higher, further dysregulating our thinking and other actions. Figure 2 demonstrates how our appraisals, judgments, and expression of our experience may flip back to increase our arousal, just as our arousal makes our thinking more judgmental and negative. The good news is that this interaction gives us two places to practice more effective alternatives.

Conflict Patterns in Relationships

Over time, all couples develop fairly consistent ways of interacting, or patterns, in conflict situations. These patterns may vary by topic or situation, but they are often quite consistent. Again, "conflict" here simply means situations of apparent disagreement, situations in which at least one partner doesn't like something the other is or is not doing, or situations in which negotiation or agreement is desired.

Constructive Engagement Pattern

This is, of course, the goal: Partners bring up issues that bother them when they are relevant, and they do so in a nonaggressive, descriptive, and clear way. The other partner listens, tries to understand, and communicates that understanding even when she or he disagrees. This allows many problems to be solved and for partners to learn increasingly how to be better mates for each other. And, importantly, when problems can't be solved, either because no solutions are available at the time or because partners continue to disagree, in a constructive pattern, partners can tolerate the disagreement, box it up (at least temporarily), and enjoy each other in other situations. In fact, being able to explore the conflict can bring couples closer, increasing mutual understanding and smoothing out bumps in the relationship. Clearly, both partners must be able to regulate their emotion, and must be aware of their wants, preferences, emotions, opinions, and what they like and don't like. Because their emotions are regulated, they are able to express these things accurately and nonaggressively and are able to listen and respond nondefensively, with empathy and validation.

Mutual Avoidance Pattern

In a mutual avoidance pattern, partners dysregulate each other. That is, when one partner experiences something negative and starts to get upset beyond a certain point, the other perceives the rising emotion and starts to spike emotionally as well. Then, each person, cognizant of the other's high negative arousal and potential for dysregulated responding (ineffective, invalidating, getting angry, and so on), avoids bringing the issue up at all. Of course, problems that can't be discussed can't be solved. And when partners feel relief when not talking with each other, an avoidance pattern can start easily. Closeness fades, even though active conflict (arguing, fighting), per se, may be infrequent.

Destructive Engagement Pattern

In contrast to the avoidance pattern, here partners end up expressing a lot of hostility, fail to remember or express their love for each other, and are unable to understand each other's point of view (which is, naturally, obfuscated by inaccurate, often hostile, expression). By the end of every argument both partners have behaved badly and will have regrets about their own actions—later, after they return to their emotional equilibrium. And, most partners will have increased vulnerability to emotional reactivity in the next conflict situation, fearing both their own and their partner's responses to conflict.

It is important to note that destructive engagement does not necessarily start this way. It is so named because this is where the conversation ends up. In fact, one or both partners may start out reasonably calm and emotionally regulated, with clear awareness of their good intentions, their commitment, and their love for one another. But without the ability to stay regulated in a difficult situation, if the conflict cannot easily be resolved, one partner (and soon after, the other) will become increasingly upset and cross the line into ineffective behavior, or stop describing what he or she wants accurately, stop listening with empathy, and so forth. Sometimes the damage is minor, sometimes it is major.

Engage-Distance Pattern

Unlike the other patterns, in the engage-distance pattern, there is an imbalance between the partners: one moves one way; the other goes in a different direction. That is, one person wants to discuss or pursue a topic and be together, but the other person, at least in that moment, does not want to discuss a topic further or perhaps even be together and instead seeks some alone time. What makes this pattern particularly tricky is that the engager or distancer can start out doing so in either an effective, constructive way or a more destructive, aversive, or avoidant way, but regardless, the pattern ends up being a disaster (Fruzzetti and Jacobson 1990).

For example, if Sally had a difficult day at work, she may want to talk with Ron about it. For example, she might say, "Oh, what a day I've had!" But, at that moment, Ron might be involved with something else, and therefore he may not notice that Sally really wants to talk and get some emotional support. His response, "Hi, Sweetheart ... I've been trying to get this Internet connection to work ... but it's not cooperating," is quite invalidating to Sally, and her arousal goes up. As her arousal goes up, her focus shifts from what she really wants (support from her husband, to be listened to and feel close to him) to her own arousal, which was already elevated due to problems she had during the day (emotional vulnerability). Then, she tells Ron, "Never mind," in a slightly nasty tone. Ron, still a little oblivious, takes the "never mind" content seriously and feels a relieved: Sally is irritated, and it's difficult and often unpleasant to talk with her when she's irritable. So, he cheerfully says "Okay" and goes back to what he was doing. Sally goes to the other room and starts stewing in the negative arousal that resulted from this additional "failure" on Ron's part to be responsive. She starts feeling overwhelmed with emotion (her original emotion plus hurt, sadness, shame, and anger), negative appraisals ("he really doesn't care about me"), judgments about Ron ("he's so selfish"), and/or judgments about herself ("it's my own fault; I'm such a jerk for thinking he'd be interested"). A few minutes later, now dysregulated, she yells at Ron, "I don't even know why I stay married to you" or "I don't even know why you stay married to me." Ron now reacts defensively (his own arousal just shot up), saying something like, "Why would I want to talk with you? You're acting like a crazy person! All I've been doing is trying to fix the damn computer, and you're acting like I committed murder or something!" Both partners feel let down by the other and will have increased sensitivity going into the next conflict situation. There are many ways this pattern can develop, but escalated negative emotions are always at the core of this destructive pattern.

How Negative Interactions Affect Individuals

Research has shown repeatedly that being in a healthy, close relationship is good for people (e.g., Brown and Harris 1978). Similarly, being in a distressed or highly conflictual relationship takes its toll on individual well-being: For example, people are much more likely to be depressed if they are in a distressed couple relationship than in a happy one (Fruzzetti 1996). Similarly, rates of substance abuse, anxiety disorders, health problems, and so on are markedly higher among distressed and high-conflict couples (Whisman and Uebelacker 2003). In addition, high-conflict relationships have deleterious effects on children who are regularly exposed to parental conflict (e.g., Cummings and Davies 1994; Gottman and Katz 1989). Importantly, research has also shown that when couples resolve their difficulties and improve their relationship, individual well-being increases substantially (e.g., Jacobson et al. 1991; Jacobson et al. 1993). There is something about being able to express ourselves and be understood, about companionship, about closeness, about being able to find peace with our partner, which seems to salve our souls.

Using This Book

This book is about learning to manage your emotions effectively in order to promote better communication, foster love and closeness, and solve problems. It is based jointly on principles of dialectical behavior therapy, a treatment for severe and pervasive problems of emotion dysregulation developed by Dr. Marsha Linehan (1993a, 1993b; see also Fruzzetti 2002), and principles of couple and family interaction and intervention developed by many in the field of couples therapy, including the author (e.g., Fruzzetti 1997; Fruzzetti and Mosco 2006; Fruzzetti and Iverson 2004; Fruzzetti and Iverson 2006; Fruzzetti and Fruzzetti 2003; Fruzzetti, Hoffman, and Santisteban, forthcoming; Fruzzetti and Jacobson 1990; Hoffman, Fruzzetti, and Swenson 1999; Hoffman et al. 2005).

This book is intended for couples in high-conflict relationships or who have enough conflict to be worrisome, or to warrant taking an active role in trying to improve your relationship. This book may also be very useful for couples who do not seem to have a lot of conflict but who in fact avoid conflict or conflict situations because these situations typically escalate. However, one caveat is needed: if high conflict in your relationship includes physical or sexual aggression or violence, this book is not intended to be enough for you. If you have been aggressive or violent with your partner, it is important for you to use all available resources to create safety in your relationship; please, seek out professional counseling and/or other resources to help you gain this kind of self-control. If you have been physically or sexually assaulted by your partner, please seek out support and resources to help you make your relationship safer: no one deserves to be physically or sexually assaulted. The phone number for the National Domestic Violence Hotline is 1-800-799-SAFE (7233); you may also visit the organization's Web site for more information and to access other resources (http://www.ndvh.org) or call your local crisis service.

The ideas and strategies in this book are designed to be helpful, but they do involve doing things together and talking about topics or issues that may be provocative because of your own and your partner's previous experiences and sensitivities. It is essential that both partners have the self-control and the commitment to self-control to tolerate such potential distress without becoming aggressive or violent. Only then can the resources of this book be truly helpful.

Ideally, you and your partner will read this book together, practicing skills from each chapter as you go along. But, of course, you (and your relationship) likely could benefit from reading the book and practicing most of the exercises on your own. Each chapter provides a step-by-step guide to identify areas that need work, as well as areas of strength, and gives practice exercises—some that you can do individually and some practices that you can do together as a couple.

The book's chapters probably should be read in order. The materials and skills are designed to build forward and cumulatively. Although in principle you could skip ahead, mastering earlier skills will make later skills easier and the likelihood of success greater. More importantly, this book is intended as a guide for practice even more than a guide to understanding. The benefits you accrue from this book will very likely reflect how much you practice the various exercises and skills provided. Although it's fine to read ahead, you might consider practicing the material in each section before moving on to the next section. For example, you might spend a week or more on a chapter

before moving on to the next chapter.
In summary: practice, practice, practice!

Chapter 2

Accepting Yourself and Your Partner

Couple interaction has often been compared to a dance: When the music flows, the timing is right, and partners know their own steps and are aware of the other's steps, it can be magical. But, when anything is off, partners begin to step on each other's toes and the activity is anything but fun (and can in fact be very painful). The painful outcome then inhibits dancing to subsequent tunes. Being an effective partner, in dancing or in other ways, requires practice and skill. Being an effective couple or team requires practice together. And, just as in dancing, a partner needs to be both an individual, doing his or her part, and an integral part of the couple. In fact, when partners are very skillful, part of the fun is letting go of self-awareness and instead participating in the joint or collaborative activity. This can be true in conversation, on a walk, or while making love.

Basic communication has two fundamental parts: one person talks; the other listens, understands, and responds. Then, at various times, partners change roles. It sounds simple, but as discussed in chapter 1, negative emotions get in the way of this seemingly simple two-step. One of the first places where communication breaks down is when we make it more complicated in our minds, increase our emotional arousal, and then go on to rationalize how reasonable it is to treat the other person badly. Acting skillfully requires an awareness, or mindfulness, of ourselves (our wants, thoughts, sensations, emotions), mindfulness of the other person (his or her wants, thoughts, sensations, emotions), and finally mindfulness of how we are connected to each other (our interaction). Mindfulness primarily involves awareness, and as a skill, it means learning to pay attention to things that matter to us most, and using that awareness to direct our actions (Bishop et al. 2004; Brown and

Ryan 2003; Fruzzetti and Iverson 2004). This chapter will explore all three of these facets of mindfulness: our self, our partner, and our joint interaction or dance together, starting with how infinitely connected we are to our partners.

You Cannot Act Alone: Awareness of Connection

In any partnership, the things we do as individuals affect the other person and the relationship. In a couple, if one person is distressed about something, it is also the other person's concern, whether he or she acknowledges it or not. *Reciprocity* ensures that you cannot act in isolation, that what you do affects the other and, in turn, what the other person does affects you. Putting the two together, you see that what you do comes back to affect you. Philosophers, poets, religious leaders, mystics, politicians, and sports junkies have all understood these axioms for centuries: "What goes around comes around," "you get what you give," "give and you will receive," and "burn and be burned" all capture the essence of this idea. Nowhere is this more true than in an intimate relationship.

Don't Soil Your Own Nest

Because we are so completely connected to our partner, it makes sense not to treat the other person badly, for we'll be treated badly in return. In order to treat our partner in a harsh, unloving, critical, or invalidating way, we simply have to "forget" or be unaware of this reciprocity. High emotional arousal, remember, reduces our thinking and recall skills, so this lack of awareness in conflict situations is not as silly as it may sound. Yet, it may be very important.

Notice your level of emotional arousal right now. If it is low or moderate, notice how you feel toward your partner, your commitment to your relationship, and notice what you want out of your relationship. If your goals include having a loving relationship, notice just that. Now, ask yourself, what if you had been able to recall these loving intentions, these desires, just seconds before the last time you snapped at your partner? What if, at that moment, you were truly aware that this is a person you love and who loves you, and that how you treat him or her would go a long way toward determining whether you get what you want in your relationship? Would it have been so easy to say the nasty thing? Probably not.

Think about Sally and Ron from chapter 1. What if Sally had been able to remember her actual relationship goals before yelling at Ron? Did being nasty help her get the closeness she wanted? Might remembering her goals have inhibited her from attacking Ron? What if Ron had remembered that he loved Sally and that he wants a happy partner and closeness with her? Could he so easily have dismissed her needs? Just being able to remember the simple truism that "what you do affects what you get" can make a huge difference. Because high arousal interferes with thinking and memory, it is important for this awareness to be almost automatic. To make this kind of mindfulness automatic, however, requires a lot of practice.

PRACTICE

1. Notice how your voice tone affects the voice tone of the person you speak to.
2. Change your voice tone and see how it changes the voice tone of the other person (you may have to demonstrate the change a few times before the other person matches you).
3. When your level of negative emotional arousal is low, notice how much you love your partner, notice your commitment to your relationship, and notice the things you both want from your relationship, such as companionship, friendship, support, and understanding.
4. Notice that you are in the same boat together: you sail or sink together. Every day remind yourself about how you are connected to your partner: "Your happiness is my happiness, and your

unhappiness is my unhappiness. When I take care of your needs, I am also taking care of my own. When I treat you with love and kindness, I am taking care of myself also."
5. Notice how your mood affects others around you, and vice versa.
6. Before saying something to your partner, even in an easy, nonconflictual situation, ask yourself, "Is this going to make things better or worse?" or, if you prefer, "Is this going to get me what I really want in the long term?" Practice this one as much as possible, even several times per day. Notice how empowering it is to be able to *choose* how you proceed rather than simply reacting.

Self-Awareness and Mindfulness of Self

Mindfulness is a term that has become more popular in recent years, and has a lot of different meanings and applications (e.g., Baer 2003; Bishop et al. 2004; Brown and Ryan 2003;

Fruzzetti and Iverson 2004; Nhât Hanh 1975, 1987). This section will focus on the aspects of mindfulness that involve our ability to be self-aware and those that involve being able to control what we pay attention to as a way of managing our emotions and our actions.

States of Mind or Self

Our *thinking self* and our *feeling self* can work together, or they can work at cross purposes. Or, to put it differently, when we are aware (and accepting) of both our emotions and our logical thoughts, we are more likely to act effectively. The various combinations of logic and emotion result in three somewhat different "self " states, or states of mind. Dr. Marsha Linehan (1993a, 1993b) has described these states as "emotion mind," "reasonable mind," and "wise mind."

Emotional Self or Emotion Mind

We need emotions to survive and to thrive in the world. Emotions orient us, tell us how important things are, signal us about the likely consequences of actions, and allow for complexity and intensity in our relationships and other activities. Without emotions, we could not enjoy anything, like or dislike anything, care much about anything, or be in love. However, when we pay attention only to our emotion and are unaware of logic or reason, things can be risky. Acting exclusively from emotion, in some situations, means acting from urges without regard to consequences. This is our pure emotional self, or a state of *emotion mind* (Linehan 1993a, 1993b). The problem with our pure emotional self is not that our emotions are strong but that they are not in balance with logic, and our actions are more like reactions, only focused on satisfying immediate emotion-based urges.

Logical Self or Reasonable Mind

Of course, we also need critical thinking, logical analysis, and reason, often in the form of shorthand rules. Without rules, chaos would reign. Logic tells us to drive on the right (in North, Central, and South America, continental Europe and Scandinavia, anyway), get up and go to work, exercise, and pay taxes. But, sometimes we operate exclusively from rules and logic and get stuck in them. For example, we come up with faulty rules, such as "I should like someone who likes me" or "only lazy people stay home with a common cold," or use logic (or pseudologic) to decide how to act, such as "if he loves me, he should know what I want, so I shouldn't have to say." The problem is not that these rules lack logic. Indeed, some rules might work a good deal of the time to keep your life organized. Rather, the problem is that they are out of balance with emotion and that our actions are then rule-driven, without regard to the consequences. Then, the rules often end up in opposition to the reasons for having rules in the first place, to reduce pain and chaos and enhance our lives, and instead increase misery.

Wise or Balanced Self, or Wise Mind

When logic and emotion are both present and balanced, we can think of this as a wise or balanced perspective. Linehan calls this *wise mind* (or, sometimes, *wise self;* 1993a, 1993b).

When we are "in" our wise mind (balanced reason and emotion) our actions are consistent with our wisest goals, and are less reactive. Often, people suggest that logic and emotion are opposite. However, in this view, they are simply different things. Much as we would say that protein and carbohydrate are both necessary parts of our diet but could be out of balance, we would say that logic and emotion are both necessary parts of our experience and ourselves. There is nothing illogical about emotions, and nothing unemotional about logic; they are simply different systems. When we have sufficient amounts of both, we can act wisely. Sometimes we think of this perspective as our authentic or genuine self, and it reflects a kind of clarity and centeredness about who we are, what is truly important to us, and what is in our hearts.

Everyone has the capacity for such wisdom. You know what temperature you like your bath or shower. You don't need to scald yourself or conduct an experiment with carefully calibrated thermometers to know you like it warm, cool, or hot; your toe or elbow just "knows" when it's the way you like it. You know that your actions affect others, and vice versa. And you know in your heart how truly committed you are to your relationship. It is important to note that what is wise will be different for different people: For some, four parts logic plus one part emotion is what is needed in a given situation; for others, seven parts emotion and two parts logic would be effective in the same situation. Consequently, there is no such thing as being "too emotional" or "too logical" if the one is balanced with the other sufficiently to get you acting effectively in your life, neither reacting (not enough logic to balance effectively) nor following rules blithely (not enough emotion to balance effectively).

When your wise self "knows" that you want your relationship to work, you are informed by both your investments in the relationship (logic) and your attraction and love (emotion). If that is your wise self, then when you have urges to hurt your partner, you are coming from your hurt emotional self (out of balance), and when you tell yourself that your partner "should" act in a certain way or he or she doesn't love you (ineffective rule), then you are coming from your logical self (also out of balance). When acting from your wise perspective, your actions are very likely to be effective: you are then most able to get what you genuinely want without hurting others and without sacrificing your self-respect.

The key skills to learn, of course, are how to recognize when you are not in your wise mind and how to get back to it.

Getting to a Balanced Self: Describing and Not Judging

There are many ways to orient your attention in a difficult or conflictual situation. You can interpret a situation, judge it, numb out or run away from it, engage in a lot of other activities to avoid it, or get stuck in your emotion about it. These are typically ineffective strategies. Alternatively, you can notice the situation and your reaction and describe it. *Describing* is one of the most effective ways to get to a more balanced place, to interrupt rising reactivity, and to keep yourself from acting in ways that make things worse (cf. Linehan 1993b; Fruzzetti and Iverson 2006).

Describing sounds simple, and when arousal is low, it can be easy, although there are some pitfalls. You can describe things outside yourself, such as the room around you, the temperature of the air, or the colors and textures of a painting or photograph. Or, you can describe things inside yourself, such as sensations, emotions, wants, or thoughts.

When we describe, we are intentionally not imposing an emotional quality to what we are describing. Instead, we are allowing our emotion to occur and accepting what might come up. Whatever emotion flows naturally from describing is likely to be quite authentic.

A prototype for description is what an event announcer does on the radio: he or she describes the activities going on, giving enough detail for the listener to understand the situation. When we simply describe situations, we notice details and put words on them, including noticing aspects of the situation or another person, as well as noticing and describing our reactions (emotions, sensations, likes and dislikes, and so forth). For example, when you are washing dishes, you can simply notice and describe how the water, soap, and dishes feel in your hands, describe the process of cleaning the dishes, and so on (Nhât Hanh 1975). Or, when your spouse or partner tells you that he or she loves you, you can notice and describe the situation (partner's tone of voice and facial expression) and your reaction (warm feeling inside, relaxing muscles in your face or neck, perhaps a smile appearing on your face).

The Problem of Judgments

What makes describing difficult to do in a conflict situation is that arousal is high, and judgments fly out of high arousal almost automatically. Judgments identify things or people or their actions as right or wrong. One problem with making judgments is that logic tells us that things that are wrong must be stopped. But, typically, the things we judge are simply things we don't like. We want them to stop or be different, but they are not necessarily wrong.

For example, Oscar stayed late at work to finish something that he thought needed to be done before he left. Maria missed Oscar all day and wanted him to come home about the same time she got home, around 5:30P.M., so they could spend time together. Oscar left Maria a message that he would be late, probably home around 7:00P.M. Although she was initially disappointed he would be late, she started judging him for it: "He's always staying late. He shouldn't spend so much time at work. He should be more interested in me." Soon thereafter, as her arousal went up, she also started judging herself: "I don't know why I'm so upset, it's no big deal. He's out there working hard, I have no right to be upset with him for being a little bit late. There's something wrong with me for being so needy." As time wore on, she went back and forth between judging Oscar and judging herself, each time increasing her arousal. Finally, around 7:30P.M., she just got stuck on "Oscar is a jerk; he just shouldn't be so late" and found herself being very angry at him when he did come home a few minutes later. Consequently, when he arrived, she complained about the situation and criticized Oscar in a fairly hostile way. Oscar was looking forward to seeing Maria despite being tired and hungry. However, as soon as she started criticizing him, he felt attacked, quickly became defensive, and started being judgmental himself, asking, "how dare she treat me this way?" They had a fairly long and nasty argument for several minutes. He then left the house and went to get dinner at a fast-food place. Maria ate dinner alone at home and went to the bedroom where she sobbed and eventually fell asleep. When Oscar came home, he flipped on the TV and watched in the dark for a while, then went to sleep on the sofa. This example shows how dangerous judgments are. Judgments boost emotional arousal and lead to dysregulation, far away from balanced and effective action.

Secondary Emotional Reactions

Notice in the example that judgments transformed each partner's initial, fairly modest, and totally valid emotion into something much bigger and destructive. Normative, adaptive, and effective emotional reactions, especially those that arise from observing and describing a situation, can be thought of as *primary emotions* (Greenberg and Johnson 1990). These kinds of emotional reactions typically are universal, such as feeling disappointed when we don't get something we want, fear in a truly dangerous situation, or contentment when things go our way. In contrast, *secondary emotions* are those that either are triggered by judgments or are reactions to primary emotions (Greenberg and Johnson 1990; Fruzzetti and Iverson 2006). Secondary emotions are less likely to be normative and typically are problematic and/or maladaptive. For example, Maria was really longing to be with Oscar and disappointed that their time would be shortened, but her judgments about him led her to be very angry at him, and, intermittently, her judgments about herself led her to feel ashamed of herself.

This highlights several important things about secondary emotions: they are almost always destructive in relationships; judgments about yourself lead to the secondary emotion of shame; judgments about others lead to anger; and big secondary emotions simply fuel more judgments, so the cycle naturally escalates.

The Problem of Anger in Relationships

Many people argue that anger is a normative and often healthy emotion, that it motivates us to stick up for our rights, values, boundaries, and helps protect us in dangerous situations. This all may be true, but there is a very corrosive aspect to anger in close relationships that often overshadows any possible benefits. For purposes of this discussion, anger is *not* synonymous with annoyance, dislike, or frustration. It can be healthy and constructive to express those emotions in close relationships, because that kind of expression can reasonably be heard and understood and can result in positive changes and increased intimacy.

In contrast, feeling angry means having increased negative emotional arousal; this in turn churns out judgments. Judgments then increase arousal, which produces more judgments, which leads to inaccurate and ineffective expression of emotions and desires, which then results in misunderstanding and conflict (see figure 2 in chapter 1), and rarely leads to effective changes. Thus, angry feelings and angry expressions in close relationships almost always create distance, and distance is the enemy of closeness and intimacy. So, what is the alternative when you don't like something?

The Power of Description

Description(cf. Linehan1993b) has the power to defuse this destructive cycle of judgments, negative arousal, misunderstanding, and conflict. If we can describe the situation, describe our reactions (sensations, emotions, wants), and notice how our reactions make sense, most often our emotions will be soothed, and we will return to a more balanced perspective, and then act effectively (Nhât Hanh 1975, 1987). One benefit of the strength of anger is that it is easy to notice, and noticing anger can become a signal or alarm that we are going down a destructive path. We can learn to notice this alarm and can respond by, first, reorienting our attention to look for judgments, second, letting judgments go, not giving them power, and third, turning our attention to description instead. After our anger has dissipated, we can then act more effectively, which at that point will be much more authentic and easier to do.

If Maria had noticed herself becoming judgmental, she could have stopped and described. She would have noticed that her husband, Oscar, was working late and she missed him. She would have noticed disappointment that he hadn't come home earlier and could have also realized how sensible missing him and feeling disappointed were in that situation. Chances are, her emotional arousal would not have escalated, and she would not have been overwhelmed with judgments, negative thoughts, and anger. She simply would have felt disappointed. She then could have reoriented herself to doing other things until Oscar came home. Then, with her negative arousal (disappointment) being fairly low, her natural and authentic reaction to seeing him (joy, relief, and other positive emotions) would have been able to emerge, not having to compete with judgments and anger. She then could have expressed her joy at seeing Oscar: she would have smiled, quite automatically, because she would have been able to notice that she was getting what she wanted. He likely would have responded to this very positive stimulus (Maria smiling and loving him rather than Maria criticizing and attacking him) in a very loving way (smiling back, giving her a hug, making warm eye contact). They could have gone on to enjoy their evening together fully.

PRACTICE

1. Practice just noticing your own experience, without judgment. You can do this in the shower (just

notice and describe how the water, soap, and shampoo feel) or by simply noticing what it feels like to breathe (the experience of the air entering through your nose, its temperature, how it feels in your nose and throat, the experience of your lungs expanding and contracting, how the air feels as you exhale). If you are tired, notice and describe the sensations. If you are happy, notice where in your body the sensations are different, how happiness manifests in your body, face, and muscles. Don't try to change your experience: just notice it, describe it, experience it.
2. Practice identifying judgments and sorting out judgments from description. For example, when you think, "That's a beautiful painting," you can try to practice (beautiful is a judgment): describe the qualities of the painting (subject, colors, texture, pattern) and notice your reactions (warm feeling, makes you smile, reminds you of something of value to you, enjoyment). Notice how your

reactions make sense, given what you are paying attention to. Try this with both pleasant and unpleasant things and emotions.
3. When you notice a judgment or notice anger, try to describe the situation and your reaction without judging. Start with easy situations that have nothing to do with your mate, and then gradually practice with negative judgments and anger (again, not involving your partner). Finally, when you are alone, try this practice on something your partner did about which you are angry. Notice how your arousal comes down when you describe.

Mindfulness of Your Partner

When you pay attention to your partner, you may similarly notice and describe—that is, you are mindful of him or her—or you may evaluate and judge. Judging is easy, and our culture supports it wholeheartedly. It's easier to say somebody is a wonderful person, or an awful person, than to describe their actions and your reactions. In reality, this shorthand communication works fairly well, if we recognize that it is, indeed, shorthand and not literally true. When your partner does something you like, she or he is not a wonderful partner. When your partner does something you don't like, he or she is not an awful partner.

The judgments we make take us away from our actual experience: "wonderful" is a concept, an appraisal, and it may interfere (at least a little) with simply feeling close and noticing your reactions to something your partner did that you liked. Similarly, the judgmental label "awful" creates anger, which gets in the way of genuinely noticing your feelings (disappointment that your partner didn't do what you wanted). Disappointment is generally not pleasant to experience and is not culturally sanctioned as much as anger, which is embraced and supported by our culture and society. Yet, anger is toxic to our close relationships, whereas disappointment is not only authentic but also can be part of a healing process. Thus, being able to be mindful of your partner requires that, on occasion, you be willing to simply feel disappointed. Of course, at other times, there will be many positive emotions and experiences.

Notice and Describe

When you are mindful of your partner, noticing and describing (without judgment) is the core of the activity (Linehan 1993b; Nhât Hanh 1975). When you notice the expression on his face (which muscles are tight or relaxed, the position of his eyebrows and the corners of his mouth), the way he walks, the tone of his voice (its pitch, cadence), and simply describe these things, you are being really mindful of him. When you notice and describe how she holds your hand (which fingers touch, how strong the grip is), the pattern of her breathing while she sleeps (deep or shallow), or the way she looks up over her eyeglasses to answer a question, you are being mindful of her.

Noticing and describing often are open and lead to curiosity, wanting to understand more, whereas judgments and appraisals are closed, not open to further information (judgment has been rendered). When you assume what his feelings are, interpret or evaluate her response, question his motivation, or focus on how illogical she is being, you have stopped paying attention to your partner, lack awareness, and are not being mindful of him or her. Mindfulness of your partner is the gateway to listening and understanding, and eventually to collaboration, support, conflict resolution, and closeness.

Again, this is often difficult to do because we are primed for conflict: arousal rises quickly, and judgments may have become almost automatic. Consequently, we have to practice long and hard to unlearn destructive patterns (judgments and rapid negative arousal). You can start by slowing down, and reorienting your attention, using skills from the earlier mindfulness practices. Be aware of your long-term goals and notice your own experience. Continue to describe and allow your experience (sensations, emotions), without judgment, until you are more or less at your emotional equilibrium point. Then, turn your attention to your partner: describe his or her facial expression (where her eyebrows are, how open his eyes are, how much tension you see in her cheeks, whether his lips are open or closed); posture (position, direction she is leaning, whether his shoulders appear tense or relaxed); hair (how long it is, its color, where it sits or falls); attention (what she is paying attention to, how intensely involved he is). When you are simply noticing and describing, you are also communicating that you accept and love your partner.

Similarly, you can be mindful of what your partner is saying. This is often more complicated, because our logical minds immediately respond to another person's words and we begin to interpret, evaluate and/or judge. However, you can practice noticing what the other person is saying, how he or she is saying it, and really try to describe what your partner is communicating (what she thinks, what he feels, what she wants, what he was doing).

Being mindful of another person while she or he is talking (active listening with openness) can be a potent way to validate someone, which will be discussed more in chapters 7 and 8. For now, it makes sense to focus your practice of mindful listening to nonconflict situations. Subsequent chapters will cover how to use these skills in conflict situations.

PRACTICE

1. Notice and describe your partner when she or he is doing something near you but in which you are not involved (reading the newspaper, playing with your child, folding laundry, sleeping, walking by). Stick with descriptions, and try not to get stuck in evaluations, judgments (good or bad, right or wrong), or your own reactions. Notice your reactions, but bring your attention back to your partner quickly.
2. When your partner is talking to someone else, notice and describe what he or she is saying, thinking, wanting, and feeling, and base your observation only on what he or she is saying (no interpretations).

3. When you and your partner are discussing something that is positive or neutral to both of you (not a conflict situation), practice mindful listening: do not think about what you are going to say next; instead listen for understanding. If your partner is not saying what he is feeling, thinking, and wanting, ask. Focus all your energy on describing what she or he wants or feels or thinks and on understanding these things about your partner.

Chapter 3

How to Stop Making Things Worse

The previous chapter provided some important building blocks for turning around the negativity and reactivity that sometimes overwhelm your relationship. Before you can make things a lot better, however, you have to stop making things worse. This chapter will focus on generating the motivation to stop making things worse, how to interrupt your own negative responses, and how to inhibit your urges to do things that you later realize are destructive to the relationship, or at least how to ride those destructive urges out without acting on them.

Get Committed to Being Effective

The first step toward self-control is commitment. By definition, when you are out of control (throwing the proverbial fuel on the fire), you are not using logic (or any other helpful process) enough. Commitment means practicing alternative reactions ahead of time until they become automatic. Then, as you start to become out of control, this new automatic behavior appears. In a way, commitment gives you self-control.

If you wanted to run a marathon, but you had never run more than three kilometers, you couldn't do it. No matter how much you wanted to keep running, you would be unable to merely will your body to perform in that situation. You would have to really want to run the marathon, which would get you out of bed early every day for months to work out, to practice. With enough commitment, you would engage in enough practice so that when your body started to fade, you could keep on running effectively (despite the pain).

But, even if you have the capacity to do a particular behavior that is effective, you might still lack the motivation. Perhaps the old problem reaction is there, too, competing with the new one. You might react either way. In situations of high negative emotion, when it is harder to do the new behavior, you are likely to think, "I don't really care about that." In this emotional state, you fail to see the consequences of your actions. So, getting to a balanced place in your mind, one in which you are broadly aware of your real relationship goals and not just your painful emotion, is important. Practicing now, so you can get there in situations of duress, is essential.

If you learned to drive on the right-hand side of the street, and you took a vacation in a country where they drive on the left, you would know, on the one hand, that it is very dangerous to drive on the right there. On the other hand, you probably would have strong urges to pull to the right. How would you get yourself to drive safely? Through commitment (remembering it really is safe, and practicing even though it is difficult), plus mindfully observing your urges instead of giving in to them or believing them (even when they scream at you), and you would coach yourself through it.

Self-Righteousness Is Not "Right"

Let's start with your commitment *not* to make things worse in your relationship. Do you really see how being nasty, invalidating, or critical toward your partner, *no matter what she or he just did,* will only make your relationship worse? Or, do you think that when he or she does these kinds of things to you that you have a "right" to respond with similar behavior (that she or he "deserves it")? Most of us know it is not effective to be nasty. But there are times when we get judgmental and self-righteous. The trouble here is that so much of our language and culture supports us in escalating when someone has "violated our rights." It is no surprise that we then describe things in terms of right and wrong, even with our loved ones.

However, if you truly adopt a mindful stance toward your partner, you will see that you are both doing the same thing. She or he thinks you deserve it, and you think your partner deserves it. How could this possibly be resolved unless one (and eventually both) of you steps back mindfully and see that, as Gandhi said, "an eye for an eye leaves the whole world blind"? Do you *really* want to hurt your partner? You know how much she or he hurt you. Do you really want to cause that much pain to your beloved?

So, use the mindfulness skills from the last chapter. Recognize that, in your heart and soul, you love this person and want to get along better, not worse; that hurting him or her is hurting yourself and continuing the unending agony of reciprocal retribution. You can stop it.

PRACTICE

1. Focus on the consequences of continuing to fight. Notice the consequences of attacking back. Of course, it is painful when your partner verbally attacks you. Recognize that by responding in kind, you are almost guaranteeing more volleys in your direction, the

negative cycle will continue, and you will find no peace.

2. Think about a specific thing you did in a recent argument to make things worse. Really notice how what you did, however reasonable in a right-wrong sense (ordinary conversation), made things worse and got you less of what you really want (peace, less conflict, more love). Practice this several times, each time recognizing the folly of thinking that you had a "right" to act that way.

Stepping Out Is Not Surrender

Maybe you now are thinking, "It's surrender to be attacked, and not to attack back!" Well, refusing to continue to fight to the death (of your relationship) is hardly surrendering. Rather, if defeating your partner is also self-defeating, then stopping the fight is both showing the courage to do what is needed to survive and the courage to engage in self-preservation without harming your partner. You can get out of "winlose" thinking (which really means "lose-lose") and into recognizing that not attacking is a win-win-win situation: you preserve your self-respect and your relationship and your partner emerges less trampled. Nobody loses.

If you think that stopping is surrender, you will likely feel ashamed, for we are typically taught to "stand up for what is right." But, if you realize that stopping requires courage, conviction, and skills, and will lead to a better life for everyone involved, you will see that shame is not justified. Rather, feeling proud seems more in order. Notice how proud you can be about your self-control and about your commitment to self-control.

PRACTICE

Practice imagining yourself stepping back when your partner is verbally attacking you. Notice how you are acting according to your values, in a way that is much more likely to result in you getting what you want and your partner getting what she or he wants (love, closeness, understanding). Try to feel a bit proud of your courageous act.

Anticipate Your Impulsiveness

Even if you are highly committed to stop making things worse in conflict situations, you still need to practice a host of skills needed to stop. When we are in the middle of enduring a verbal attack from someone else, our own reaction feels impulsive, like an unpredictable and overbearing urge. However, realistically, a lot of these situations are quite predictable. How many times have you had *that* fight? How many times has your partner said that particular hurtful and provocative thing? Look descriptively at previous problems: what did your partner do that resulted in your emotions going through the roof to the point where you had urges to retaliate? We will call those things *triggers* because they trigger your response.

Rehearse a New Emotional Response

Once you have identified typical triggers, you can anticipate that your partner will say them again. The more aware you are of the triggers, the less potent they will be. In a way, every time you imagine your partner saying that trigger and imagine that you respond in a kind way (or, at least, not in kind), you are reconditioning the trigger because you are changing the cycle. So, identify as many triggers as you can.

The idea is not that these triggers *cause* your response, but rather that the cycle is now automatic (she says X, you say Y; he says A, you say B). It's a learned habit, much like reciting the alphabet. If someone literally says "A, B, C, D, E, F" and then suddenly stops, years of practice may cause you to say "G" in response. But imagine that you find out that saying "G" now causes an explosion! You need to stop saying "G" and do something else. What else? The effective thing to do is anything that brings your arousal down and helps you respond differently, of course.

There are many strategies for tolerating distress in dialectical behavior therapy (DBT) that might be helpful in these situations (Linehan 1993b). For example, you can distract yourself away from the argument by doing something else (take a walk, read, engage in other activities that are physically active ones or relaxing ones), look for spiritual soothing (say a little prayer, remember your values), do something soothing to your senses (listen to quiet music, eat comfort food, read a pleasant story or poem), or do something social (call a friend, send an e-mail). Some of these things you can do quickly, in many situations. Others you will simply have to plan to do after successfully ending the interaction without responding negatively. Just knowing that you will have a few minutes to focus on feeling a bit better may help you respond more constructively.

Once you have identified the typical triggers and also identified more helpful alternatives, you can put them together.

Imagine a trigger, imagine remembering your goal (not to make things worse, that you love this person, that responding in a negative way just keeps the negative cycle going), and imagine responding in a self-respecting and respectful way.

PRACTICE

1. Identify as many triggers as you can for your impulsive reactions. Write them down.
2. Come up with a list of things that you can do immediately, while under verbal attack, to tolerate it without attacking back. What can you say to yourself? What can you focus on? What would be distracting (from your urge to retaliate) or soothing (of your fraying emotions)?
3. Now, practice putting these things together. Imagine the trigger and then imagine that you provide the alternative, less hostile, and more constructive response. Keep practicing.

Rehearse Ending the Conflict Gracefully

One of the biggest problems with being upset or overwhelmed is that we can't think well. We often cannot find useful words that would make the situation better, so we end up on autopilot, spewing out the same destructive responses that have not worked in the past. Chapter 9 will discuss some of the finer points of this issue. But for now it is probably sufficient to actually memorize a line or two that will help you end the conflict gracefully.

Some possibilities to consider include the following:
- Observing that you are fighting and disclosing that you don't want to
- Disclosing that you are sad or feel some other primary emotion
- Disclosing that you love him or her and don't want to continue down this negative path
- Disclosing that you care a lot about your partner and want to understand, but are overwhelmed right now

- Suggesting that you take a break and come back to the conversation later

Of course, whatever you say needs to be in your own words, but the essence of an effective response is staying reasonably calm and describing something about your genuine goals and feelings rather than telling the other person what she or he is doing wrong.

Edgar and Selena fought in such a nasty way that it took days for them to recover to the point where they could even look at each other. Each one had acquired the ignoble skill of knowing just how to hurt the other, which buttons to push to create the most suffering and biggest reaction. Of course, hurting the other was not their goal. In reality, they longed to return to the earlier form of their relationship when they were each other's best friends, could count on each other for soothing and support, and had a lot of fun together.

Edgar knew his triggers were exactly the things he could expect Selena to say. He was committed to changing his response, but he would become tongue-tied when he was really hurt, sad, and angry. After another broadside, he would inevitably respond in the same old negative way, and things would just deteriorate. But, since he knew in advance more or less what Selena would say that would act as a trigger, he decided to plan what he would say in response. He wanted an effective way to stop the argument. He decided to say, "Selena, I miss you. This fighting is so hard on me. I just don't want to do it anymore. Can we take a break and come back later when we're both calmed down and can be nicer?" He rehearsed it over and over. But when the time came, he was surprised at how hard it was to resist the urge to yell back at her. Having practiced, he managed to ride out the urge, remembering their good times together and his commitment to turn their conflict around. When he finally got the words out, he was a bit surprised and very relieved that Selena agreed. They interrupted what was sure to be another three days in hell and instead started down a very different path toward understanding each other and being with each other.

Manage Destructive Urges

Commitment and practicing alternative responses are very helpful in achieving self-control. But there are other skills you can use when urges to do harm are running high.

Did you ever have the urge to eat more dessert and not do it? Did you ever have the urge to stay in bed rather than go to work, the gym, or school, but you managed to get up and go anyway? How about urges to buy things you could not afford, run away rather than face a difficult task, cheat on your taxes, steal something, lie about something to avoid someone's anger or disappointment, or drive a car while intoxicated? What other irresponsible or destructive urges have you had? Have you always given in to these urges, or have you managed them and done what was needed in those situations (at least sometimes) to make your life work?

Whatever you did to resist those kinds of urges are important skills to use when resisting the urge to treat your partner badly and continue the destructive conflict cycles you sometimes get in. Below are three common strategies to help you respond without making things worse in a difficult situation. You may have others that work as well.

Visualize the Negative Consequences of Giving In to Your Destructive Urges

If the alarm clock goes off and you are tired, comfortable and snuggling with your sweetie, you may have the urge to turn it off and go back to sleep. But, you remember that your boss is not too pleased when you simply fail to show up for work. You realize that you will be swamped for the next several days trying to catch up on what you don't do today if you stay home. You remember that your performance appraisal hinted at the possibility that you do not put a lot of effort into your job, and you remember that you have $17 left in your checking account. Within a minute or two, you are in the shower and have forgotten about that cozy and relaxing bed that is still being kept warm by your spouse or partner. What happened? You remembered the negative consequences of following your urge instead of doing the wise thing. Or, to put it another way, you wisely balanced the short-term benefits of behavior (cozy bed and partner for a few minutes) with the shorter plus longer-term costs of that behavior (angry boss, risks of losing your job or not getting a raise, financial peril, personal shame). This method can be very effective at motivating us to act in ways that are responsible to our own longer-term goals.

Step Out and Observe the Urge

Alternatively, after the alarm clock goes off, you could observe your own behavior. You might notice that you often feel strong urges to stay in bed, especially when it is dark out and your sweetie is still there. You might then notice that by not immediately taking the urge to stay in bed too seriously (observing it rather than going with it), the urge is already subsiding.

Interestingly, when we observe urges, they often lose their potency. Perhaps you have noticed that sometimes an advertisement on the TV or radio just screams at you, and you feel an urge to do what it's saying ("you must watch our show tonight at ten o'clock" or "you are not being a good parent if you don't buy our product"). However, as soon as you notice (observe, remember) that the advertisement was developed to get you to spend your money on a product, the immediacy of the urge falls away. Maybe you will, maybe you won't. You can decide rather than react. Observing behaviors is a very powerful way to let some of the emotionality out of our reactions, and urges are nothing if not reactions.

Visualize the Positive Consequences of Riding Out the Urge

Once more, go back to the example in which you have urges to stay in bed when the alarm clock goes off. At that point, you may be able to get yourself to think about your day ahead. If you do, you might realize that you have an enjoyable project to work on and that you are saving money for a down payment on your first house. You might remember that several people at work are counting on you, that you really like being part of a team, and that you like several of your coworkers. Again, in a minute or two, you will be in the shower and on your way.

The difference between this example and visualizing the negative consequences of giving in is that the former uses your motivation to avoid negative consequences, whereas this one uses your motivation to achieve positive ones. Both can work rather well in the moment. To which do you respond better?

In nasty, negative situations with your partner, use whatever strategies work for you. Maybe remembering that you will cause your partner and yourself a lot of suffering if you respond in that automatic, nasty way will help. Or, perhaps thinking about how lovely it is when things are going well will help you stop your "madness." Or, maybe observing yourself in the middle of this scene will give you the motivation to change the dialogue from what you previously recited, and redo the ending.

PRACTICE

1. Practice visualizing the positive and negative consequences of both your old, automatic negative response to your partner's triggers and your new, more neutral or constructive responses.
2. Practice observing your urges in a variety of daily situations. How do you ride them out? Identify what typically works for you and figure out how to use that strategy when in a high-conflict situation with your partner.

Chapter 4

Being "Together" When You Are Together

When couples have a lot of conflict, closeness wanes and partners begin to avoid doing things together. And, even when they do things together physically, they often are not "together" emotionally, but rather are on red alert for signs of impending conflict, hypervigilant to anything the other does that might signal dislike, disapproval, or further distance. Or, they simply ignore each other, turn inwards, and engage the world alone, even if their partner is sitting across the table or lying next to them in bed. In this chapter, the focus will be on finding ways to bring your attention to these moments when you are physically together, letting go of negative emotions and negative thinking, letting your guard down, and being together when you are together.

Getting Yourself Oriented to Being Together

Sometimes you may find that there has been so much conflict between the two of you, so little positive interaction, and so little affection, that you both show up to situations defensively, or ready to fight, even before anything happens. This means that certain situations themselves have become *conditioned* to lead to escalating negative arousal, regardless of what you or your partner does in those situations. For example, if you have had regular arguments about household chores, parenting, sex, money, how to spend time together, and so on, just being in a situation in which any of these topics is present may be enough to result in conditioned anger, apprehension, and lots of negative judgments about your partner ("he's going to unfairly demand…" or "she's going to wrongly do…" or "she's not going to do what I want" or "he's going to criticize me") or yourself ("I'm going to mess this up"). In these situations, it may be effective to work on *reconditioning* difficult situations before you enter them. Fortunately, this is a relatively easy thing to do.

Conditioning and Reconditioning

Emotions are either *natural reactions* to situations, and thereby normative and predictable, or *conditioned reactions,* and therefore not normative in those situations and not predictable to those unfamiliar with your relationship. For example, talking about who is going to pick the kids up from school when they only have a half day is often stressful for busy parents who are both employed. So, it is normative and predictable that one or both partners would be stressed when the topic comes up. However, anger and resentment might be the emotion that one or both partners express. This likely means that in previous similar situations the discussion turned into an argument that was not resolved well, and hurt feelings, disappointment, and frustration were felt. Being judgmental probably turned those feelings into hurt and anger, over time if not right away. Now, in this or related situations, anger is immediate, before any negotiation takes place, even before anyone speaks.

In order to proceed effectively, it is important to bring more balance to this situation. One way to do this is to recondition the situation so that it triggers a more normative emotional reaction and intensity. This can be approached in a number of ways, but perhaps the most efficient is either to have a consistent place (physical location) or a specific, tangible stimulus that evokes opposite emotions.

Conditioning a Place to Recharge and Get Balanced

Find a place in your house that is comfortable. It should evoke no negative feelings and should be a place where you have not had arguments or retreated to when upset. Rather, it should evoke calm, comfort, and peace. It might be a room, but it could simply be a favorite chair or even a particular pillow or cushion you put in a sunny spot on the floor, or near a window or heating or cooling vent. If you go there every day for a few minutes and think about your partner mindfully, think about how important he or she is to you, how much you love him or her, after not too many days, this place will become associated with warm and loving feelings toward your partner. This is your relationship spot. The idea is to actively condition this location to be your place to recharge your energy about your partner, your relationship, and your marriage. It is better to go somewhere else when you are upset to comfort yourself when you need to. This spot should be for one thing and one thing only: thinking about and experiencing your partner in a loving way.

Like any "charging" station, you can only take away as much energy as you put in. If you regularly use this spot to contemplate your partner in a loving and mindful way, you can return to this spot when you want to recharge just prior to entering into a difficult situation. Just by going there you will be telling yourself, reminding yourself, of the many good and important things about your partner and relationship that you know and feel in your heart, but that easily can be overshadowed in difficult situations. This location is like shining a bright light on what is in your heart but hidden in the shadow of your anger. Your love and commitment are really there; you just have to illuminate them and look in that direction to find them, to be reminded of their presence and importance.

Conditioning a Relationship Box, Album, or Book

An alternative to creating a relationship charging station in a particular location is to create something tangible that evokes similar emotions and thoughts. This might be a scrapbook, photo album, or box, a kind of holding area for things that remind you of the wonderful characteristics of your partner and the genuine meaning of your relationship to you. Into this scrapbook or box, you can put potent reminders of your partner, your love for each other, and of shared experiences you have enjoyed. These might be photos from fun activities, your wedding or honeymoon, or photos of your partner with one or more of your children. Or, it might include ticket stubs from fun events you attended together, stubs from boarding passes from an airplane, train, or boat trip, a lock of your partner's hair, a picture of him or her as a child, a piece of jewelry that he or she gave you (for example, your wedding ring), a fortune from a fortune cookie that you shared, a box top from her or his favorite cereal, a birthday card from your partner, a letter, e-mail, or post-it note in which your partner told you that she/he loved you (or why), or anything else that evokes love and the commitment to making that feeling paramount instead of fear, hurt, and anger.

Just as with the relationship spot described above, this relationship reminder scrapbook or box needs practice and attention. Remember that it only has one purpose, to help orient you toward balance and effectiveness. If you spend a few minutes regularly, even daily, practicing being mindful of your partner while looking through it, the relationship reminder will become even more potent at evoking warm and loving feelings and the commitment to staying mindful, in the moment, and not escalating negatively. Over time, this set of relationship-oriented keepsakes will become effective at helping you get to your heart, your true self, about your partner and what you want in your relationship.

Showing Up Ready to Play, Not to Win

Once you have conditioned a place or a set of tangibles, you have a very real aid to counterbalance the negative conditioning that has taken place in the past months or years. You can use these aids in a number of ways.

First, you can simply use them daily to help stay mindful, balanced, and to provide genuine loving balance to the conditioned negativity that has become frequent. If you spend a few minutes in your special spot or with your reminders, then your love for and commitment to your partner, as well as your partner's love for and commitment to you, will be more salient, more palpable. Difficult situations will be less likely to overwhelm you and cast a shadow over your genuine wants and desires about your relationship and your partner. Consequently, you will enter difficult situations with your partner with less apprehension, less reactivity, less conditioned negativity.

Alternatively, you could use your aid quite purposely for a few minutes just prior to going into a difficult situation. If you know that you have to discuss who will pick the kids up at noon on a workday, and you have had many arguments and lots of negative emotion about this topic before, you might go to your spot or find your reminder and use it to shine the light of mindful awareness on your commitment to working things out, your feelings of love for your partner, and the knowledge that even in conflict, your partner loves you. Then, with balanced emotion, you can have the conversation you need to have, starting from a balanced place and not overwhelmed by prior negative conditioning.

PRACTICE

1. Create a relationship scrapbook, box, or album (or related aid) as described above, and spend focused time with it daily.
2. Alternatively, pick a "recharging" spot for relationship mindfulness, as described above, and practice daily.

Different Ways to Be Together

Despite being lonely, when partners are distressed, they often turn away from each other. They do this physically, emotionally, verbally, cognitively, and biologically (with drugs and alcohol) across all the domains of their relationship. Yet, this distancing easily can be missed because so much of it occurs inside people and is simply a function of their attention. Thus, increasing being together may mean spending more time together, but more importantly, it means being cognitively and emotionally together when already physically together (and even when not physically together), whether you are doing things together or not.

Get Into Your Own Life

The essence of being together is using your attention and your nonjudgmental awareness as a way to focus on what you have that is enjoyable, pleasant, or satisfying. However, not paying much attention has its rewards: you can avoid (sometimes, for a short while) noticing things that you don't like. But avoidance carries with it a huge cost: like an intense drug habit, we have to feed it more and more and work harder and harder to avoid. Soon, the things we do to avoid unpleasantness may create more problems than we had initially: the avoidance "solution" is often far worse than the problem (feeling bad). So, we need bigger distractions, more noise, faster games, more intense experiences, louder TV commercials, more, more, more to buffer us from whatever pain we might have (or be afraid to have). Peace and quiet may be rare. The more we distract with things that are not truly important to us, the worse our lives become because we are spending less time doing and experiencing the things we have and can do that are truly meaningful and important to us.

What things get in the way of your ability to focus your attention on the things that really matter to you? It may be useful to take a look at them. How do you escape and what are the costs? If you do want to be together with your partner, you might consider turning off the TV (for an evening, or maybe for a week or longer) or unplugging yourself from other electronic devices. You could stop drinking alcohol or using other substances that interfere with your ability to be in your own life, or at least stop long enough to see what difference it might make. The point is not that all of these things are wrong. Of course not. But, even activities and diversions that are relaxing, enjoyable, and harmless in some situations could become bad habits in other situations, and you may end up living your life in diversions. Then, what you are diverted from is your life, which includes yourself and your loved ones.

PRACTICE

1. Make a list of the things that you do to relax, to escape the pressures of your day. Evaluate the list critically. Are you using these diversions successfully or abusing them? Are they helping you to fully experience your life, or distracting you away from your life? For any that are interfering in your ability to be aware and present in your life, commit to reducing your use of those activities or habits. Try to be more mindful and use diversions to enhance your life, not escape from it.
2. The next time you are eating a meal with your partner, take a few seconds every few minutes to notice that your partner is there, eating, sitting, being together with you.
3. If you fall asleep after your partner or wake up before he or she does, take a few seconds to notice that you are in bed together, sharing the same bed, same blankets, and each other's heat. Just notice how

it feels to be lying and sleeping together (even if you are not touching each other in any way) rather than sleeping alone in the same bed.
4. When you both are doing things around the house (doing chores, getting ready for your day in the morning, getting ready for bed, reading the newspaper), take a few seconds to be aware of your partner; notice what she or he is doing and that you are together in your life.
5. Think of another opportunity to practice being more mindful of your partner. When do you typically fail to notice your partner? Practice this exercise (being aware of or describing your partner) during these moments.

Being Together Passively Vs. Actively

Even partners who are unhappy in their relationship and engage in a lot of conflict typically spend a lot of time in each other's presence, physically being in the same house or the same room, quietly sitting at the same table or on the same sofa, or sleeping in the same bed. Yet, during these times, they may not interact with each other and, more importantly, may not focus any neutral or positive attention on each other. This can be considered being *passively together.* In fact, even when doing things that seem together, like taking a walk or watching the same television show, or eating dinner at the same time at the same table, partners may be thinking about other things, not noticing or paying attention to the other person. This is a passive way to be together. Although being together passively does not itself promote difficulties, each of these situations is a lost opportunity to practice being together in ways that soothe loneliness, reduce negative reactivity, and foster closeness and togetherness.

In addition, being together passively can be risky: partners may begin to focus a lot of negative attention on each other inside their own heads, running a list of negative past deeds or anticipated negative future reactions through their minds, privately judging or criticizing the other, becoming upset and eventually going on "red alert," waiting for the other to do something and then snapping at him or her verbally. This can easily become constant, and then becomes a state of hypervigilance, which is exhausting.

Alternatively, you can be aware of each other's presence, notice what each other is doing, and feel a lot more collaborative and a lot closer emotionally whenever you are in close physical proximity (same house or room), whether you are doing something cooperatively or separately. This alternative practice reduces stress and can improve the ambient emotional climate, and it entails very few risks.

The idea is to use the relational mindfulness skills from chapter 2, such as increasing awareness of the other and letting go of judgments (increasing nonjudgmental awareness) in any situation in which your partner is physically present, whether in the same room or even the same building. The idea is not to think, not to interpret, not to judge the other, and not to spend time and energy noticing what your partner is *not* doing (that you might prefer). Rather, the idea is to simply notice your partner's presence and to notice what he or she is doing that is observable and describable.

For example, your partner might be in the shower while you are getting dressed in the morning. You can simply notice that she or he is there, in the same or next room, getting ready for the day. The only words in your head that are needed are descriptive: "I am getting dressed and he/she is in the shower." Just notice that you are here together in your day and in your life. Or, maybe she or he is reading the newspaper while you are watching television, reading a book, or playing with one of your children. Again you can notice and describe: "He/she is sitting over there, watching a show and smiling (or attentive, or looks bored)." Perhaps one of you is cleaning up after dinner while the other is washing dishes, playing with the kids, doing some chore, or just relaxing. Rather than simply focusing on your own activity, or being critical and judgmental about what your partner is doing (or how he or she is doing it), you can simply notice that you are together in the same room or house, and notice and describe what he or she is doing. If you find yourself thinking, your mind wandering into the litany of complaints you have about your partner (or worrying or resenting the complaints you imagine your partner has about you), just catch yourself and redirect your attention back to noticing what is actually present, what he or she literally is doing. Just notice and describe. Just this enhanced awareness, along with *not* being critical or judgmental, is wonderful practice and brings you closer to being actively together.

Being *actively together* means occupying the same emotional space, letting your judgments and criticisms go (at least temporarily), and allowing yourself to appreciate or enjoy each other's company. There is no need to put pressure on yourself or each other to do or say anything. You simply do whatever you are doing but simultaneously make sure that some of what you are aware of is your partner being there with you, living his or her life with you, at least physically.

Of course, if your partner is willing to practice this skill too, there may be times when each of you is quietly aware of the other: you will be secretly appreciating your partner while your partner secretly appreciates you. Imagine how lovely this could be, even if you were not even to acknowledge it out loud. Being together when you are together reduces loneliness and soothes our emotions, leaving us less negative and less reactive when somebody decides to talk!

Being Together While Interacting

Partners face myriad situations when they literally must do things together, such as doing household chores, managing children (ordinary interactions or misbehavior), visiting friends or family, engaging in sexual activities, or generally coordinating family life. Of course, most of these situations also involve negotiating and talking, which can be anxiety provoking if you have a history of conflict. Some of these times are generally positive, but in high-conflict relationships, they may still be affected by negativity and may not be experienced as positively or as fully as they could be.

Conflict Situations

In conflict situations, the default mode of operating leaves us ready to fight, ready for the other person to misstep, ready to criticize or be criticized, or, occasionally, even ready to give up and disregard what we want in order to avoid conflict (but then hang on to lingering resentment that the other person got her or his way). This is not being together.

For example, Keisha and Warren had regular disagreements about who should do what around the house. When arguing, each perceived the other as begging out of his or her responsibilities, unfairly leaving more for the other partner to do. Often, these disagreements escalated into very angry exchanges, sometimes in front of the kids. These arguments became so chronic, so hostile, that Keisha and

Warren often avoided each other out of fear of further conflict. Or, one would do a chore but resent it the whole time, thinking "I shouldn't have to do this. She/he should be doing this." Of course, each noticed only the chores that he or she completed, not those that the other did. Keisha would clean the bathroom, thinking "I'm always the one who has to clean this disgusting mess around the toilet. Warren never does it. It's not fair." Warren would clean the refrigerator, thinking "I'm always the one who has to clean this disgusting mess that drips all over the shelves. Keisha never does it. It's not fair." Needless to say, neither one noticed the hard work the other was doing and certainly never verbally acknowledged, much less appreciated or thanked, the other for his or her efforts and accomplishments. So, when it was time to clean up after having friends over for dinner, each would think the other "owed" him or her some work and would hang back a little rather than make an effort. This, of course, proved to each partner that the other was lazy. Consequently, cleaning up often ended up in another argument that devolved into name-calling ("you're lazy" and "you're irresponsible" were common epithets), and the hurt feelings and negative emotions would then carry over into other activities.

The alternative to reacting, allowing your emotions from and judgments about past situations to dictate your reactions, is difficult, but it is essential in creating more harmony and dissipating fear and resentment. It involves finding a way to be together in the present, even when negotiation is required and conflict likely. The first step has to do with thinking about and experiencing yourself as partners, as part of a partnership, as a team, not as opponents or adversaries. This involves moving toward a regular experience of yourselves as "we" as opposed to "you and me."

In any conflict situation, the first step is to become purposeful, aware of what you each are doing and what the situation is. Start by describing the situation, then notice and describe your own experience (thoughts, comfort, emotions, sensations). Then notice and describe your partner. What is he or she doing physically (standing, sitting, and so on)? What is his or her facial expression? Notice that you are doing something together. If it is a situation in which you have had conflict in the past, notice that you bring apprehension to the situation, which your partner can probably feel or see (even if he or she is not fully aware of or does not acknowledge this). Take a deep breath and recognize that the situation will go better if it is allowed to be unfettered from the previous conflict. Let your worries go. The worst thing that can happen is that you will have another argument (not pleasant, but not uncommon), and chances of this are decreased, not increased, by letting go of your apprehension and just being in this moment, here and now.

Warren and Keisha just had another dinner party, but now each has read this chapter. As Warren starts to clear the table and bring dirty dishes into the kitchen, he is flooded with apprehension and with thoughts that Keisha "probably will leave most of the work for me. It's not fair." But, he catches himself, realizing that Keisha is actually clearing the table, too. He decides to try to be present and let the past go for now. He notices that Keisha looks tired. Yet she is scooping up dishes and cups and taking them to the kitchen. He remembers that she made most of the dinner while he was pouring drinks and hanging out with their friends as they arrived. He appreciates the lovely dinner Keisha prepared. He appreciates that even though she is tired, she is cleaning up. Even though he may be cleaning up more quickly, he realizes she is probably more tired than he is. He notices how nice she looks, that in fact he finds her very attractive. He is able to smile at her as she comes back into the dining room for more dirty dishes. He notices that she smiles back and seems relaxed and glad to be with him.

After their friends left, Keisha had an urge to go to the bathroom for a while to avoid trying to clean up together. It was not that she minded cleaning up. No, the issue was that they frequently have had arguments in these situations, and she was tired and wanted to avoid having another argument. She started thinking, "I always have to do these chores, and I resent it. I made dinner while Warren did nothing but have fun, so I should be able to sit and relax now." But then she remembered that they both had pledged to work on noticing each other, slowing down, and "being together" when they are together. So she decided to try to just notice Warren and work on the chore together. Then she remembered that, in fact, he had vacuumed the living room at the last minute before their friends arrived (it looked so nice) and had served drinks and hors d'oeuvres while she was making dinner. She noticed that he was cleaning up and at first seemed a little grumpy or maybe on edge. But she kept noticing that he was energetically moving back and forth between the kitchen and dining room, efficiently carrying lots of dirty dishes into the kitchen, putting them in hot soapy water, and then coming back for more. After a few trips, he seemed more relaxed. She kept working, too, and felt closer to him as she noticed they were working as a team. Neither of them said anything. But, she just melted inside when he smiled at her as she left the kitchen and returned to the dining room, and she beamed back at him, feeling much less apprehensive and, in fact, much closer to him than she had all evening.

As you begin to engage in an activity together, keep your attention in the present. What are you doing? What is your partner doing? Stay descriptive, immediately letting go of judgments, analysis, or other thinking. Stay focused: Keep your attention on the task itself or on noticing each other engaging in the task, without any evaluation of yourself or your partner. Notice any warm feelings. If you do notice negative feelings or find yourself drifting into judgments and criticisms or worry thoughts, simply bring your attention back to noticing and describing yourself, noticing and describing your partner, and noticing and describing the activity in which you are both involved. Repeat as necessary!

This exercise is extremely difficult, but it allows you to engage in a joint activity with less escalation, less chance of acrimony, and a greater chance of being together in your interaction. This is also a skill that you can practice in your imagination. Rehearse noticing and describing in your mind *before* the activity, so you are primed when you actually start. Of course, you can combine this skill with the relationship mindfulness aids discussed earlier (relationship spot or relationship reminder). Later chapters will discuss applying these principles to conversations and more extensive interactions and negotiations.

PRACTICE

1. Think of a difficult situation that you had recently that resulted in a fight. In your mind, reconstruct the situation and go through it again, only this time practice being more skillful. Stay descriptive, stay in the present (let go of judgments, thoughts about previous conflicts), and notice your partner and describe what he or she is doing. Notice you are doing something together. Keep rehearsing your new

skill in your mind until you can get through the difficult situation reasonably easily.
2. Now practice being together in a real situation in which you feel a little bit apprehensive. Stay mindful: notice and describe with no judgments. Keep practicing.
3. Finally, practice "being together" in a more difficult situation, using the same skills. If you drift toward judgment, criticism, anger, fear, and negativity, just notice that you have drifted, take a breath, and start again.

Enjoyable, Nonconflict Situations

The last aspect of being together when together has nothing to do with conflict but instead focuses on situations that are still enjoyable or could be enjoyable if you approached them a bit differently. It may be that because other things in your relationship are troublesome and there has been a lot of negativity, you find that you hold back a little bit even in pleasant, enjoyable, or even intensely exciting situations. These are situations in which it may be desirable to be even more together when you are together.

The same principles and skills pertain to these situations, but surprisingly it may be more difficult to remember to use them, even though this situation is not toxic or conflictual. However, fully engaging in fun things together is more fun, more enjoyable, and has more lasting rewards, so it is worth the effort. These situations include doing fun recreational activities but also might include doing things with your children, parents, or other family members, playing games together, cooking or doing other activities that are fun to do together, holding hands, kissing, hugging, making love, talking about fun topics, planning activities, or anything else that is enjoyable. All of these activities are more enjoyable when you are experiencing them together and are fully present (your attention and awareness are focused on the given activity).

Again, the skill is to bring your awareness fully to the present situation.

Notice and release any worry thoughts, any withholding of enthusiasm, any judgments of yourself or your partner. Really bring your attention to the activity, paying close attention to how you are feeling and how your partner is reacting, and finally, to how the two of you are interacting. Allow yourself to be awash in the good feelings; don't truncate them or suppress them, and don't *think* about them. Just feel them, enjoy them, notice them, and participate in the feelings and the activity. Repeat as often as you can! We will revisit this issue again in chapter 5 when we look at reinvigorating your relationship, and again in chapter 11 when we focus on closeness and intimacy, but now is the time to get started practicing this "being together" skill.

Being Together Even When Physically Apart

Finally, it is important to keep your partner in your awareness and your heart even when you are not together. Thus, it is important to think about your partner during the day or night when you are not together. However, rather than letting certain negative situations or stimuli dictate what you feel, it is important to be proactive and purposefully set aside a minute or two several times a day to focus your attention on things about your partner that you love, appreciate, respect, make you feel close, or value about him or her. Simply think about your partner doing one of these things (playing with your child, smiling at you, touching you lovingly on the shoulder, working hard at his or her job), and notice your feelings. After thirty seconds or a minute, just go back to what you were doing.

PRACTICE

1. Monitor your positive feelings during the course of the day. Start with all of the positive feelings you might have, in any situation, not just those that have something to do with your partner. Try to notice your experience, and in particular notice if you are holding back from fully experiencing any positive

feelings. If you are holding back, try to let go and just feel what you feel more fully. Allow yourself just to "be" in the experience, neither trying to hold on to it nor trying to push it down or minimize it.

2. Now focus on monitoring your positive feelings toward your partner over the course of the day, even when you are not together. Again, simply notice warm or positive feelings when they occur and try to allow them to develop fully, neither intentionally trying to make them bigger than they actually are nor trying to minimize them.

3. Over the course of the day, while you are not with your partner, try to recall something that you love or value about your partner, and let yourself feel lovingly toward him or her. Be mindful of your partner and your feelings about him or her. Practice this several times each day.

4. In a situation in which you are actually with your partner and notice positive feelings (warmth,

love, affection, appreciation, desire), really focus your attention on those feelings. Then focus back on your partner and go back to your feelings. Keep going back and forth, and notice what happens.
5. Try to initiate small situations in which you can be together emotionally. Pick several things you can do that do not require extra time or preparation, things that you might do in the course of your day, like holding hands, rubbing noses, standing or sitting together to watch your child do something across the room or through a window. Just notice and enjoy being together. What could be better than mindful conversation, mindful parenting, mindful hand-holding, mindful sex, or mindful sunset watching with the person you love?

Chapter 5

Reactivating Your Relationship

Early in your relationship, chances are that you did things together that were really enjoyable. These may have been activities that you would have enjoyed doing with anybody, or maybe they were things you did that were special because you did them together. However, as conflict grew and tension mounted, you may have stopped doing these fun activities; indeed, maybe you have stopped or curtailed many activities together. The pleasant, fun, close times that resulted from shared activities became fewer and farther between, and you have lost some energy and enthusiasm for each other. Maybe it has even seemed like your relationship is withering away. The purpose of this chapter is to help you start to reactivate and reinvigorate your relationship, doing more things and spending more time together, helping your relationship to thrive again. This chapter also will focus on how to better appreciate the time you spend apart by sharing your independent experiences with each other. And, it will focus on how to reactivate your relationship by doing more loving, caring, and considerate things for your partner, without any strings attached.

Enjoying More Time Together

Now that you are more aware of physical proximity and emotional closeness, more able to be aware of your partner and your interactions together without these moments escalating into blame and criticism, and more able to enjoy time you do have with each other, it is time to engage the world more, together as a couple.

There are several different domains that many couples find important to their life together. Not everyone finds each domain equally important, and it is not necessary to share activities across all areas for couples to be satisfied and healthy. What follows are some different types of activities that many couples enjoy sharing. It is likely that you have enjoyed time together doing some of these things in the past, although it may have been some time ago. Within each type of activity, consider both what you might have done in the past that was satisfying (with or without your partner), as well as what could become satisfying in the near future. Remember, the more varied your set of activities, the better. Novel situations and activities keep our minds stimulated and our lives interesting. You can start by making a list of what you'd like to do, and maybe your partner can also make a list (see the practice exercises below), and then you can start to do more things together. Keep an open mind, and be adventurous!

Increase Social and Family Time with Others

Identifying yourself as half of a couple or marital union is an important thing to do. But this identity must be based on real, shared time together doing things as a couple. Some of those kinds of activities involve socializing as a couple with friends and extended family. Of course, there is nothing wrong with socializing as a brother or sister with your siblings, or as a son or daughter with your parents, or alone (without your partner) with your friends, coworkers, neighbors, and so on. However, it is also important to do things as a couple, in which you identify yourselves as a couple, and those with whom you are spending time also see you as a couple.

It is healthy to have a part of your identity tied to your partner as part of your union together. The only way to create or strengthen this "coupleness" identity is to practice. You can go out on a double date with another couple, visit family as a couple, hold a BBQ as a couple, go to a wine or chocolate tasting together (or host one), and so on.

However, while you are doing these social activities, it is important to notice and enjoy that you are doing them together as a couple, to be mindful of the activity as a joint activity, or as an opportunity to be in the world together rather than as two separate individuals.

Engage in Recreational or Fun Activities Together

Life can be hectic, and we can easily spend time doing things that we "should" do and, over time, do fewer and fewer fun things that invigorate us individually or as a couple. When time together also brings opportunities to fight with each other, it is even easier to hole up at home, do things alone or with friends instead of your mate, and let couple recreation fall by the wayside. If you have children, it can be complicated and/or time consuming to find a sitter, and hiring a sitter means that doing anything alone as a couple is expensive. Thus there are additional barriers to enjoying recreational activities together as a couple. However, doing fun things together regularly is an essential part of identifying as a couple. It gives you time to let down your guard and rekindle the experience of sharing life experiences together that are not just chores and "have to" activities. Paradoxically, this gives you more energy, both individually and as a couple.

Start a List and Keep Adding Ideas to It

You may know what kinds of things would be fun to do together, or you might not be able to think about anything right now. What is important is to start to make a long list of possibilities. You can brainstorm together or each make a list and put them together. You can solicit ideas from your friends or others, and be very creative. It is important not to focus on big things like vacations right now. Sure, vacations can be great, if you agree on where and when to go and how to spend the time, and if you have very compatible ideas and plenty of money and vacation time to do it. However, the idea here is to generate a lot of different ideas for activities that you can do regularly, perhaps daily, but at least weekly. They should not strain your budget, and you should not include items on your final list of recreational activities if the enjoyment of doing them would be outweighed by the work involved in arranging to do them.

If you have children, certainly you can include them in some of these activities, more as family than couple recreation. But it will be especially helpful if you can also identify many activities that you can do without the children, if only for a few minutes daily or for a longer period once every week or two. If you have trouble paying for a sitter, consider trading child care with a friend, sibling, or neighbor. Also, you can prioritize activities that you can do after the kids are in bed, or before they get up, or while they are with friends on a weekend afternoon. Don't give up. Your life together is too important not to figure out how to enjoy time together.

Some Ideas to Get You Started

When you brainstorm a list of possible activities, consider things that you used to do together that were fun and resulted in feeling close, gave you stories to tell others, or were just enjoyable times together. It is especially helpful if at least half of the list consists of things that cost very little or no money (or are easily within your budget). Inexpensive things to do might include going for a walk or hike. Go Rollerblading or ice-skating together, go window shopping, go to a public venue where there might be a free or inexpensive concert, exhibit, fair, or show, or read something together (a short story, poems, old letters, information about a mutual interest, the daily newspaper, or a favorite magazine). Search for information about a topic on the Internet, put old photos in an album, sing or play instruments together, or go to the library and check out music to listen to together. Consider opening up the free activities section of your local newspaper, then close your eyes and point at something at random, and go do it. Go out for coffee or breakfast, meet for lunch, go out for ice cream or popcorn, go to a movie, or go look at holiday decorations around town. You also can exercise, work out, or play a sport together. Include some things on your list that require no preparation or advance planning, so you can be spontaneous sometimes. Be adventurous and creative and include things that you might never have done, or never did before together, and especially include things that might be out of the ordinary, challenging, or whimsical. Take a risk, but remember: it's not really very risky if you do it together.

It is also possible to choose activities around your house or yard if both of you agree they seem like fun things to do. For example, you might repaint a room or wash the car together, but only if it would be fun and not a chore—and especially if you might end up spraying water at each other playfully. However, don't choose anything that either of you feels is work, any activity that either of you really doesn't like to do—or, at least, does not want to do right now. You can leave these on the list, but skip over them for now.

You can also choose some things that require preparation, planning, or cost some money. For example, there might be a favorite concert or sporting event coming up next week or next month that likely will sell out, so you would need to get tickets in advance (or save some money for it). Or, maybe you need a reservation for a corner table at what used to be your favorite restaurant to go to together. If you want to go canoeing or camping or skiing, it might require some planning and preparations, and joining a gym, racket club, or sports facility together might require budget planning. These are all wonderful opportunities to have fun together.

The idea of the activity list is to keep it fresh. Add things to the list regularly, and cross things off that turn out to be impossible to do or just are not fun when you do them. Some activities do require planning, so start well in advance of the desired date for the activity, leaving plenty of time to switch plans should your first ideas not work out. And, of course, share the preparations and advance work.

PRACTICE

1. Make your activity list. Generate a lot of ideas together, or, each of you can come up with a list and

then put them together. Keep the list fresh.
2. Get active! Pick something from the list and do it together in the next few days. Stay mindful and enjoy your time together. Do something fun together at least every week, and consider getting your relationship moving even more often. Write down times to do things together on your calendar, either specific things you know you will do together or blocks of time that you will use (you can be spontaneous on those days).
3. Plan now for a slightly bigger activity (not necessarily costing a lot of money but one that requires some advance planning). Do the planning and preparations today or tomorrow.

Share Intellect, Interests, and Ideas

Everyone has a rich life in their heads. We all have interests, ideas about the world around us, and things we are very knowledgeable about. This world inside ourselves goes a long way toward defining who we are as individuals. Some people may think about art, popular bands, philosophy, their jobs, or relationships while others may be concerned about global warming, their aging parents, the latest technology, or shoe fashions. Unfortunately, when we keep these thoughts to ourselves over long periods, our partners can lose touch with who we really are and what we think about and care about: what makes us tick. Interestingly, the fact that we initially were attracted to each other and liked each other (and still do) means that we probably either shared some of these interests and ideas or at least found the other person likable and desirable in part because of these individual interests, knowledge, and abilities. But it is difficult to be attracted to someone you don't know too well anymore, and you may feel vulnerable opening up now if you retreated a long time ago or felt criticized or invalidated for sharing these thoughts in the past.

So, now it is time to open up again, to let your partner into the world inside your head, and to foray into your partner's world too. Chances are pretty good that it will seem at least strangely familiar, and you will enjoy both journeys.

The most important thing here is to balance your mutual interest and curiosity with a recognition of each other's vulnerabilities. So, start slow. Set aside a few minutes only, and take turns talking about an idea you had or your partner had, or an interest one of you has. The other person just has to listen. Keep it short, so there is no misunderstanding, and so there is no time burden. At first, it is better to end prematurely, wanting more, than to keep talking and perhaps heighten expectations for more rather than simply gaining a new understanding about what's going on inside the other person. Maybe you read something in the newspaper that moved you (excited, saddened, created hope or despair), or you have been doing something with a hobby or pastime that the other person knows nothing about. Maybe your partner heard a new or old song by a favorite singer and really liked it. The idea is to exchange these kinds of things, just to learn a little about each other's private worlds. No big response is required; a simple "um-hmm" or "I didn't know that" or "that's interesting" is sufficient. You can like hip-hop or country or classical, and your partner can like rock or salsa or jazz. You don't have to have the same interests to be interested.

As you both come out of your shell, you can, of course, discuss these things. But before you engage in much discussion, make sure that you are feeling open, curious, and supportive of the other's point of view, even if you have a different interest or point of view.

PRACTICE

1. Agree to be more open with your partner about what you think about, what goes on in your head, and agree to be interested in what your partner thinks about.
2. Practice telling your partner about your thoughts and your life in your

head, just one or two ideas at a time.
3. Encourage your partner to share these kinds of things with you, and simply listen and show interest.

Share Spiritual Experiences and Values

Everyone has a spiritual side. Sometimes that spirituality has to do with religious values, and at other times it concerns social, moral, or personal values and preferences that are unrelated to religious beliefs or practices. Regardless of the form of our spirituality, for most of us, our values and beliefs and morals are centrally important to defining who we are. Sharing these kinds of core values is essential to sharing yourself and essential to your partner (and others) really knowing who you are.

In this domain, relationship activation means spending time together sharing your spiritual side with your partner. You can do this around a current issue (something in the news might prompt such a discussion), around child rearing (you might be faced with helping your child develop values you agree with and care about), or around a specific spiritual practice (such as praying, meditating, or doing something for someone less fortunate). You could read religious or spiritual writings together and discuss what they mean to you, talk about someone who is a hero to you and explain why she or he inspires you, discuss why you respect and appreciate, or don't like or agree with, a particular activity or behavior of a friend, coworker, or public person. Again, the important thing is to activate your relationship simply by sharing your thoughts and values from your spiritual side and listening to those that your partner shares with you.

PRACTICE

1. Make an effort to share your values, your spiritual side, with your partner.
2. Engage in some spiritual practice together (reading religious or spiritual writings to each other and discussing them), and/or participate

in some other spiritual activity together (go to a religious event or activity).
3. Listen with respect when your partner tells you about his or her spirituality or values. For now, it is important not to disagree or challenge those thoughts; just focus on knowing what she or he thinks and feels and what his or her values are. There will be opportunities for further explanation, disagreement, and exchanges later.

Initiate, Receive, and Enjoy a Variety of Sexual Activities More Often

A healthy relationship includes a healthy sex life. But, as relationship quality erodes in the face of conflict and other factors, it is common for sexual attraction and sexual activity to wane over time. Sexual desire may be low or nonexistent for one or both partners. Perhaps one or both of you got bored with sex, or maybe interest in sex diminished over time due to nonrelationship factors (fatigue due to working hard with child rearing, jobs, managing family life, managing the household, not getting enough sleep, or working different shifts). Maybe differences between you in sexual desire contribute to conflict. Regardless, an inert or significantly dampened sex life can restrain other dimensions of your lives together, and reinvigorating your sex life can contribute to significant improvements in other areas of your relationship. If your sex life could use reactiviting, the following tips may be of help.

Sex and Self-Respect

Reactivating your sex life can be tricky. For example, one of you might have been pushing for more sexual activity regularly while the other has been less interested and has resisted these advances, so the idea of increasing sexual activity might feel like "giving in" to one of you. Or, perhaps one or both of you still do not feel very close and trusting and loving (or loved) enough to completely relax and engage in intense sexual exchanges. While sex is an area in which it is important to engage intensely, you should only do things that feel right to you and your partner. If you feel inhibited, you should take that seriously. Figure out whether your inhibition is important to you and part of your sense of self-respect or if it is just a function of sexual disuse, habit, and/or past discomfort. If it's not about self-respect, it may be worth pushing yourself to do a little, focus on enjoying it, and try to let go of your inhibitions from there. On the other hand, you should not do anything that is not self-respecting.

There is also the complicated issue of sexual fidelity and infidelity. If infidelity has been an issue for either of you in your relationship, you may want to consider going to a therapist together to get some help rebuilding trust and recommitment. If trust is intact or you have successfully restored a high level of trust, sexual reactivation may be an important step toward healing the leftover hurts and moving forward. However, if trust is still tenuous and the repair is incomplete, it may be important to reestablish more trust before working on sexual reactivation.

Sexual Dysfunction

Many couples have problems with sexual dysfunction. Some women have vaginal pain during penetration (vaginismus) or have trouble achieving an orgasm (orgasmic dysfunction), and some men have trouble either getting or maintaining an erection (erectile dysfunction) or may regularly ejaculate upon penetration or too quickly thereafter for intercourse to be satisfying for one or both partners (premature ejaculation). Addressing these kinds of problems is beyond the scope of this book. But, fortunately, effective treatments are available for them. If you experience any of these problems, you should see your physician or an expert in sexual dysfunction (such as a psychologist, certified sex therapist, or marital/couples therapist) for a thorough evaluation and to learn about treatment options.

Yes, There Is More to Sex Than Intercourse

For our purposes, it is important to define sexual activity as anything that increases sexual attraction or sexual arousal in the moment. Sexual activity, therefore, includes sexual intercourse and any genital touching (orally, manually, etc.), but also could include kissing, sensual hand-holding, any bodily caressing that has a sexual element to it, cuddling in a sexual way, or even talking about sexual activities together. Thus, sexual reactivation means doing more of these things but not necessarily all of these things.

It is important to start by noticing your emotional attraction and allowing yourself to be romantically or physically/sexually attracted to your partner. Don't inhibit this attraction. Just notice it. Enjoy the fact that you have these feelings. Remember that you do not have to act on every thought, every urge, or every desire that you experience. You can simply enjoy feeling that attraction and those sensations. You also can act on those urges rather slowly. Consider passionately holding hands, really paying attention to how it feels to hold your partner's hands (while he or she does the same). This is likely to be very enjoyable and might be enough for now. Or, you could go from rather intense and passionate hand-holding to caressing your partner's neck, arms, legs, or feet. Enjoy the feelings, allow the sensations, and don't inhibit your passion or your desire. You might stop there, or you might go on to kissing each other on the lips, kissing other parts of each other's face, neck, body, or move toward genital touching.

You can, of course, go on to oral-genital contact, intercourse, or any number of related sexual activities. Whatever you do, go slowly (if passionately and intensely), keep your attention focused on the activity and on enjoying the sensations, and on noticing how your partner is enjoying the activity. It is important to focus your attention on enjoying receiving the sexual attention that your partner focuses on you. Notice how much attraction he or she feels toward you, how nice it feels to be desired by your partner, loved, caressed, kissed, held, or cuddled. Don't be afraid to talk about what you like more and like less, and always be respectful of each other's likes and dislikes.

Good Sex Requires Good Instruction, Lots of Practice

Some couples are really good at sex. They are naturally compatible, relatively uninhibited, creative, and able to be mindful of their own experience while simultaneously mindful of their partner. But, sex is also a skill much like any other. Some people aren't so naturally good at it, they aren't as creative or skillful at pleasing their partner, or they get very inhibited. Of course, in many parts of our culture, it is difficult to talk about sex, so bad habits are easy to start and difficult to break. As with any skill, you have to practice and get good feedback to get better at sex, but if knowledge is limited and communication about sex is poor, it is difficult to become an expert. Fortunately, there are many good guides and manuals designed to help partners enjoy the sexual parts of their relationship more. Look through the relationship or self-help section of your local bookstore for more information. And start talking about sex today.

PRACTICE

1. Think about sex with your partner more.
2. Talk about sexual desires you have about your partner with your partner.
3. Set time aside to be sexual. You can plan what you are going to do or not do, or be spontaneous. But allow yourself to engage in whatever sexual activity you choose in an intense and mindful way, enjoying it fully, not distracted by worries or evaluation: stay in the activity, in the sensation, in the moment.
4. Initiate more sexual activities of any kind. You can plan this in advance (set time aside or create a desirable mood) or do this spontaneously. Notice your attraction, your desire, the sensations, and stay mindful of them. Notice your partner and his

or her reactions, how he or she responds to your initiation.
5. Enjoy receiving sexual advances and participate in sexual activities initiated by your partner. Have fun! You may or may not want to do more, but enjoy what you have. Keep your attention focused on your sexual interaction. Let thoughts or worries about anything else go.

Enjoying Time Apart and Sharing Your Experiences

Okay, after this steamy last section, it's time to return to the more mundane, but no less important, area of what you do with your independent time apart from each other and how to use these independent activities to become closer to each other, instead of more distant.

Getting active in your life in a variety of activities is good for you. Activating your own behavior improves your own mood and level of energy (Addis and Martell 2004; Jacobson et al. 1996). And, paradoxically, activating

yourself independently from your partner also can strengthen your relationship, in at least three ways:
1. Having an energized, content partner means that he or she is more fun to be around and has more energy to give to you and the relationship.
2. Partners who have interests and activities apart from each other can bring their experiences back to their relationship and share them with each other, enriching each person's understanding and appreciation of the other.
3. If you have a partner who has other friends, other activities, other things to do, you are less likely to feel pressure to restrict your own activities and interests and instead are more likely to support your versatile interests.

There are three key things you must do, however, to make this work. The first is to stay balanced. That is, although it is important to become and stay active and interested in a variety of activities, it is also important to give at least as much attention to shared activities. So engage in a lot of independent activities *and* a lot of relationship activities. Don't neglect one and favor the other. Balance means doing enough of each to be satisfying (not neglecting yourself, not neglecting your partner, and not exhausting yourself in the process).

The second thing you must do is support each other in these independent activities. Don't feel threatened or left out but realize that having a wide variety of interests and activities is healthy (Campbell and Fruzzetti 2006). Supporting each other means you are contributing broadly to each other's well-being, and if you also are doing lots of things together, it will be easier to support each other's separate activities.

The final thing you need to do is talk about what you do apart from each other. Doing so builds trust and minimizes the chances that either of you will feel left out. Second, talking about these activities provides opportunities to support each other's activities. And, perhaps most importantly, talking about what you do and what you like and don't like about it, sharing your enthusiasm, and describing the things you notice and experience actually allows doing things apart to bring you closer. You learn more about what your partner likes and what motivates him or her, and you can be stimulated by your partner's growth, interests, and engagement in things that you might not be interested in for yourself or maybe don't have time to do.

PRACTICE

1. You and your partner each make a list of independent activities that you might like to do that would likely be enjoyable (alone or with friends) and share the lists with each other.
2. Discuss the idea of balance, and slowly add one or two independent activities to your weekly schedule. Engage in these activities fully, and enjoy them!
3. Be sure to discuss your experiences afterwards with each other. During these discussions (which can be

brief), be sure to disclose a lot about what made the activity enjoyable or why it was important to you, and be sure to support your partner's activities.

Doing Things for Each Other Without Strings Attached

In relationships, we need to remember to provide clear expressions of affection and to make caring and considerate gestures, without keeping score. This is one important area of relationship functioning that often diminishes over time and certainly is neglected in high-conflict relationships. Yet, you know how nice it is to get a phone message in which your mate simply says, "I was just thinking about you and wanted you to know," or to be sitting reading and have your partner ask if you would like a hot or cold drink and then bring it to you.

These kinds of small, considerate, and affectionate gestures build goodwill and often inspire reciprocal kinds of thoughtful actions. The idea, however, is to do something small and nice *just because you want to,* not because you will receive something nice in return. Thus, there should be no strings attached, and you most definitely should not keep score. If you don't feel like doing something nice, that's okay. But, consider being considerate.

You can do this formally by making a list of things and doing something from the list each day, or informally, by simply pushing yourself (and remembering) to do something thoughtful or considerate more spontaneously. The reward includes knowing that you are working on being a good partner, and you can be sure that your partner will feel the effects of your efforts, whether it seems like he or she notices or not.

What can you do? Consider anything that expresses affection, shows appreciation toward your partner, or anything that is considerate and contributes toward improving a moment in your partner's day. Smile. Give a back or foot rub. Make your partner toast in the morning while you are making some for yourself. Leave a note on the kitchen counter that says "looking forward to seeing you tonight," or do a chore that the other usually does (or nobody usually does). There is no need to buy anything or do anything out of the ordinary. These are simply small, considerate, caring expressions.

Of course, if you notice your partner doing considerate things for you, be sure to be mindful of this. You might want to say "thank you," but more importantly, be sure to take a moment and enjoy the consideration, the affection. Taking a moment to experience and enjoy your partner's efforts to be close to you will loop back and make a difference to him or her. In the same way, putting the effort out to express love and caring and consideration for your partner will have an important effect on him or her.

PRACTICE

1. Think of (and maybe write down) at least a dozen small, caring, or considerate things that you could do for your partner that you have not done lately.

2. Commit to doing at least one of these things every day, and practice it in your mind at first. Imagine doing these things even if you are unhappy with your partner at that moment. To help motivate you, focus on your affection for your partner.
3. Do one thing each day and do it from your heart, from a place of caring, not because you are supposed to. Appreciate your own skillfulness in doing this.

Chapter 6

Accurate Expression

The previous chapters focused first on reducing the reactivity and negativity in your interactions, and then dealt with cleaning up the mess created by a lot of destructive conflict: how to slow down, become mindful of your genuine wants and goals, mindful of your partner, and how to get reacquainted and reactivated. Now it is time to talk to each other, slowly and deliberately at first.

The Couple Two-Step

Effective communication includes two steps: one person expresses him- or herself accurately, and the other person listens, understands, and validates. This two-step dance continues, with one partner leading (expressing or disclosing) while the other follows (listens and validates). Of course, at various times partners switch who leads and who follows. The two-step provides the building blocks for all effective verbal communication.

The central points are, first, when expression is accurate, the other person can more easily understand, and thus validation (communication of that understanding) is easier to provide; and, second, when the response you get from your partner is validating, this helps keep your emotional arousal in check, which in turn makes it easier to express yourself accurately. And this cycle continues, as shown in figure 3.

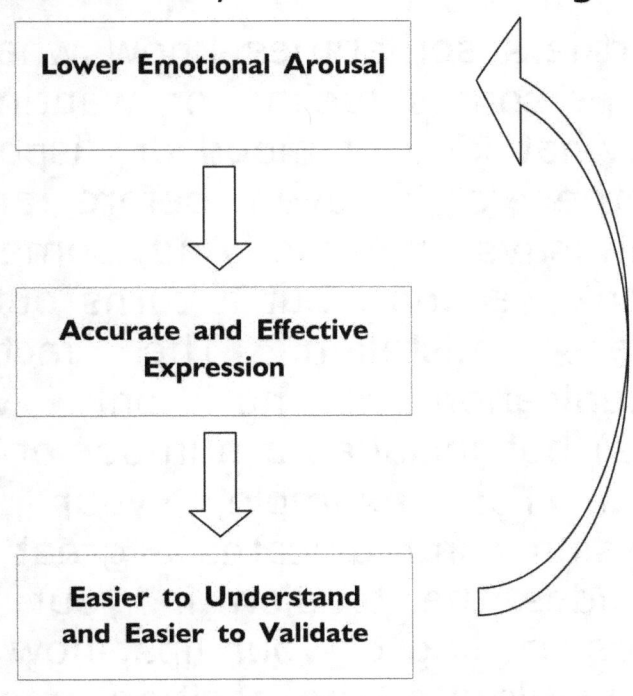

Figure 3

This chapter will focus on the first step in the couple two-step, accurate expression, and chapters 7 and 8 will focus on the second step, validation. These two steps will be expanded in later chapters into more elaborate forms designed to satisfy you and your partner in a variety of ways.

What You Bring to the Interaction: Before You Open Your Mouth

Partners sometimes know what the other person is feeling or wanting, or know what kind of mood or disposition the other is in even before anyone actually says anything. And, sometimes we think we know but it turns out that we are mistaken. The fact is, communication is not only verbal (words) but includes a number of other factors. For example, your facial expression communicates a great deal; it includes the tension in your facial muscles, curling of your lips, how open your eyelids are, the position or angles or furrowing of your eyebrows, the direction and intensity of your gaze, and the flare of your nostrils, among other factors. Body language includes muscle tension (which ones are tense versus which are relaxed), body position (leaning forward versus away), arm and leg position (folded/closed or open), movement (jumpy versus still), breathing (relaxed versus labored, sighing), and other behaviors that communicate underlying emotion quality and arousal intensity.

Any of these small behaviors can belie our emotions and expose even subtle criticism, judgments, or hostility when they are present. Even more problematic, however, is how easily even subtle facial expressions or body postures or movements can be misinterpreted. For example, if Bob feels worried about bringing up a difficult subject but tries instead to mask that worry (perhaps he even tries to bring it up differently to be more effective), Sue could easily detect the fact that he is "hiding" something, and quickly become upset about that, and criticize Bob for being "dishonest." In reality, Bob is not expressing himself accurately, even before he opens his mouth to speak. But, of course, Sue is invalidating Bob's worry and his good intentions. And, as figure 4 shows, Sue's invalidation of Bob only increases his arousal and decreases the chances of him accurately expressing what his primary emotions and genuine wants and goals are. Further miscommunication and conflict follow easily.

The road toward effective, accurate expression, therefore, begins with mindfulness. Become mindful of your own emotion (*primary* emotion, of course), let go of judgments (and negative assumptions), stay in the moment, and stay mindful of your partner. Stay aware of your longterm goals: this is the person you love and who loves you. No matter how difficult the task, the outcome will be better if you stay skillful.

If your arousal is very high, take a break and work to bring it down before you initiate the conversation. If your head is flooded with judgments ("she is too logical" or "he is too emotional" or "she/he is wrong" or "I just can't believe she/he is so stupid/insensitive/ridiculous/..."), or if your thoughts include a cascade of "shoulds" ("she should know better" or "he should not think that" or "I shouldn't have to do this"), it is time to work on being skillful. Reorient yourself to your genuine goals, describe your feelings and desires, and wait until you are in a more balanced place before initiating the conversation. It is far more effective to bring your arousal down and experience your genuine primary emotion, and have your face and body reflect that, than to try to mask high negative arousal. This is true whether that high negative arousal is directed toward your partner in a hostile or judgmental way or it is simply a reflection of your genuine (but very high level) anxiety or sadness. You will be glad you took the extra few minutes to self-regulate and get balanced before moving ahead. (Figure 4)

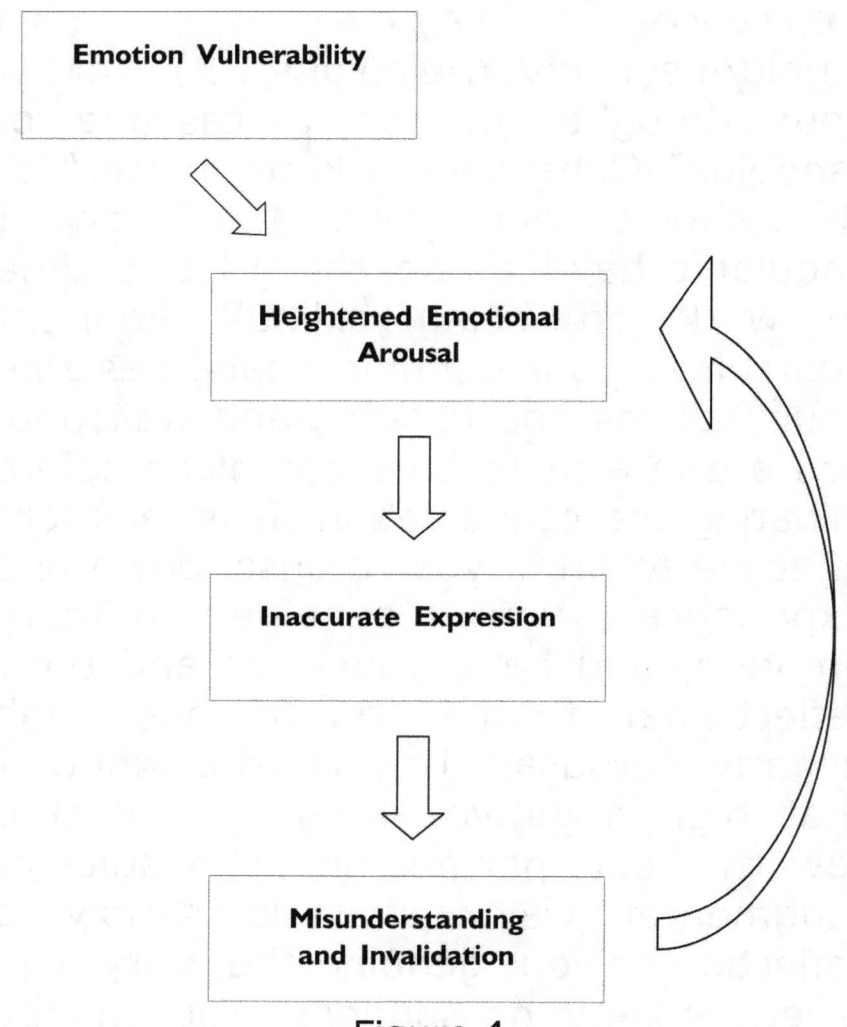

Figure 4

Take a Bathroom Break

Practicing slowing down, reflecting on your goals, noticing your arousal, and noticing what you are expressing nonverbally, can take a few minutes.

Often, partners or children interrupt these few moments, making it a real challenge to practice, and this slows down your ability to acquire this skill. However, everyone needs to go to the bathroom for a few minutes on a regular basis, and thus the bathroom affords a perfect place to practice (whether you need to use the toilet or not). Most friends and family members support your need to go to the bathroom for a couple of minutes, and they don't typically ask why. Thus, a bathroom break usually affords a few minutes, without interruption, to practice being skillful (working on mindfulness and relationship mindfulness, regulating emotion) and to get yourself ready to engage your partner constructively. Plus, bathrooms have mirrors, so they are a perfect place to notice your facial expression and tension in your face and body and to get direct feedback from your own reflection.

You can also use your ordinary bathroom breaks proactively, as opportunities to check in with yourself, noticing your arousal, your emotions, what you are doing, whether you are being effective, and whether you need to do something different at that moment to regain balance: start by simply breathing mindfully: get into the present, let go of judgments.

PRACTICE

1. Practice noticing what you bring to your interactions. Try to notice whether your facial expression and body posture reflect your real, primary emotions.
2. Try using some of the conditioning skills you practiced in chapter 4. Use your relationship reminders or visit your relationship spot to help you bring down your arousal before you initiate a conversation—even about reasonably noncontroversial topics. Notice how your partner responds differently when you are more regulated and less negatively aroused, less on alert for conflict.
3. Practice allowing your facial expression and body posture to relax and reflect your genuine feelings and desires. Use a large mirror to see the difference in what

you communicate nonverbally when you have low or moderate arousal and again when you are very upset. Don't judge yourself, just notice.
4. Practice interrupting negative arousal, taking a short break (maybe to the bathroom to practice), and using skills to experience, identify, and reflect your genuine primary emotions before initiating ordinary conversations.
5. Repeat the previous step, but do so in preparation for discussing touchy or sensitive subjects.
6. Practice mindfulness every time you use the bathroom for a few days. What do you notice? Consider committing to doing this regularly.

Know What You Want and Feel, or That You Don't Know

Once your arousal is reduced, it is easier to ask yourself the questions "what do I really want?" and "how do

I really feel?" and trust the answers. These are key questions to ask even though the answers may not always be clear.

In order to be really effective, we have to know what we genuinely think, feel, or want. It can be very useful to breathe a few deep breaths, look around, notice that there is no imminent danger or harm (hopefully!), that you love your spouse or partner, and that he or she loves you. It's usually important to remind yourself of the core of what you want: a caring, loving, supportive relationship. Even when scared, sad, frustrated, embarrassed, unhappy, and so on, these things are still true (at least if you have read this far in the book). Then, from this context (recognizing that you are physically safe, and remembering the big-picture desires of making the relationship better), you can ask these questions. When you are mindful of your true self, what is in your heart, you likely will know at least some of the answers. And, even if you don't know exactly what you are wanting or feeling, at least you will know that you are not sure, maybe are confused, or need more time to figure it out. Then, you can think about communicating what you notice: how you feel, what you want, or that you're not sure yet.

The next section will help you sort out further the wheat from the chaff, accurately identifying what your emotions and desires are generally, and avoiding common pitfalls, the things that lead us to misidentify and/or communicate inaccurately our true feelings and wants.

What Is "Inaccurate" Expression?

There are two general ways to express yourself that we might consider *inaccurate.* Both occur when emotional arousal and/or judgments are running high (Fruzzetti, Shenk, and Hoffman 2005). The first kind of inaccurate expression includes communication that really is inaccurate. For example, it might come out of cascading negative emotion in which you fail to communicate your genuine feelings but instead communicate *reactions* to those feelings (or to judgments). Or, you may be indirect or fail to reflect accurately the importance of the topic (overvaluing or undervaluing). The second type includes any number of things you might say that could be *technically* accurate but in reality interfere with your genuine goals and preclude you from saying other at least equally accurate and less hurtful things; hence, these expressions are considered inaccurate because they thwart, rather than facilitate, achieving your genuine objectives.

Expressing Secondary Emotion Instead of Primary Emotion

There are times when high emotional arousal or being judgmental transforms a primary emotion into a secondary one. When we express a secondary emotion, it is not genuinely accurate, even when it is actually what we are feeling in that moment. For example, if Tiffany misses Mark a lot and really just longs for time with him but starts judging Mark for working late, she can quickly become angry. The anger can obscure her longing, and if she simply expresses the anger (verbally and nonverbally), Mark might never realize that Tiffany just adores him and wants to be with him. He could easily become defensive in response to her anger. Instead, if Tiffany lets go of her judgments, she will quickly realize that she misses Mark and wants to be with him. If she assails him, she very likely will not get the closeness that she longs for. Instead, she will get conflict and distance. Accurate expression for Tiffany requires her to let go of judgments and notice and describe her primary emotions. Then, when she says, "Mark, I'm so glad you are home. I really missed you while you were working late!" it will come across as genuine. Mark will feel loved and be happy to be home (and may even want to come home earlier in the future). Furthermore, if Tiffany really wants Mark to make an effort to work late less often, she can bring this up in a way that he can hear, in a way that is accurate. She is asking because she misses him and wants more closeness, not because she is angry or because he is doing something "wrong." The possibilities for negotiation (see chapter 10) are improved greatly.

There are many situations in which we quickly react to our initial emotion or our initial desire, and we end up stuck in secondary emotions, forgetting our primary, genuine emotions and desires. All kinds of thoughts trigger emotions, but we often then think the emotions are in response to the situation rather than to our interpretation or thoughts about the situation. For example, Ruth was often preoccupied with the kids and with work. She was frequently quite stressed about having a lot of responsibilities. Richard was less preoccupied with those things, and just longed for a bit more closeness with Ruth. They used to spend more time together; Ruth used to have more energy and seemed to show more enthusiasm for Richard. Ruth was still very committed to Richard and also wanted to be close to him; she just didn't show it as much.

Richard's longing, his desire for more time together, more affection, and so on, really was his primary emotion. But, he sometimes had the thought that Ruth was losing interest in him, getting bored, or no longer loved him as much. With these thoughts, of course, fear crept in. Although his fear was not really justified by the reality of the situation, it was still quite painful, and was associated with a lot of painful negative arousal. Richard then started, in his mind, to criticize or judge Ruth about any little thing, which led to anger. For example, if Ruth spent time with one of the kids in the evening, Richard might think "she'd rather avoid spending time with me" and then nitpick her activities, telling himself that "she's just coddling that kid, she should know better" or that "she should have more patience with the kids" or other judgments. Of course, these judgments led to further anger and distance. Then Richard would verbally attack Ruth. Making an angry face, he would say "you need to spend more time with the kids and have more patience" or, on another occasion, "you spend too much time with them; you coddle them too much." Of course, Ruth would quickly become defensive, recognizing that she was "damned if I do, and damned if I don't spend more time with the kids." Then they would fight about parenting and eventually fight about everything. In reality, of course, both were competent and loving parents, and their fights could never lead to any resolution.

This situation is very common. Richard never communicated what he really wanted: more closeness with Ruth. In fact, paradoxically, he got less and less closeness. Through doing exercises like those in this book, Richard learned to see his anger as a red flag: he was reacting to something, and his angry reaction (secondary emotion) was obscuring things that were much more important and more genuine. His primary emotions were longing for closeness with Ruth and disappointment about their distance from each other. He learned through regular practice not to run with his anger, but to see it as a signal. When he noticed himself getting angry, he took a break and asked himself, "What might I be missing? Is there something I want that

I'm not getting (longing, disappointment)? Is there something happening or about to happen that I really don't want (fear, frustration, or dislike)? Am I fueling my anger with judgments ('right/wrong,' 'should/shouldn't')?" Richard quickly found out that he really did want more closeness with Ruth, but that he also often judged himself. He noticed himself saying, "I'm not independent enough" or "I shouldn't be jealous of Ruth spending time with the kids." He found that if he simply accepted that he felt what he felt and wanted what he wanted (accepted the reality of his feelings and desires), he could act in much more constructive ways. So, if he noticed a little longing to be with Ruth when she was off playing with the kids, he could go play with them too. Or, he could smile, give her a hug, and say something like, "Ruth, honey, can we sit together after the kids are in bed?" Ruth, when faced with this accurate communication, would usually be very responsive. It was easy for her, actually, because she often was longing for more time with Richard, too.

Making Judgments Instead of Describing What You Want or Feel

As the example of Richard and Ruth illustrates, the problem of having secondary emotional reactions is integrally connected to the problem of being judgmental. What seems to happen is each of these problems feeds the other. That is, in any situation, if you become judgmental of your partner, you will usually fuel dislike and anger. Similarly, if you feel angry, the thoughts that your brain produces under that kind of emotional arousal will often be judgmental. See for yourself: Think about something a friend or family member did that really wasn't a big deal. Now, be judgmental about what the person did (notice how it was kind of stupid, that she or he should have known better, that it was wrong to do that, and so on). What do you notice? You probably started to get angry, especially if you bought in to the judgments. The reverse is also true. The next time you find yourself feeling angry, notice what kind of thoughts you are having. Are they laced with judgments? If so, try using the technique covered in chapter 2 of *describing* the situation and your sensations and primary emotional responses. What happens to your anger?

Just as importantly, think about how it feels when someone else is judgmental toward you. How do you feel? How do you react? Being judgmental about someone you love is very hurtful to them and corrosive to your relationship.

The issue here is not that you should never be judgmental or angry. Instead, the issue is the extent to which being judgmental interferes with your genuine reactions, interferes with getting what you genuinely want, and interferes with your relationship with your spouse or partner.

Fortunately, the antidote to being judgmental and to relationship and individual suffering is being descriptive. The good news is that this same skill, being descriptive, is also the way to express yourself accurately. Review chapter 2 if you want more practice developing this skill.

PRACTICE

1. Try to notice when you are getting angry. Is anger really justified in this situation? Is it really the only emotion you have? What other emotion might you be missing (sadness, disappointment, anxiety)?
2. If you are angry, notice if you have been judgmental in your mind or just said something judgmental. If so, try to let go of the judgments and notice what other emotions you might be feeling. Notice the situation and describe your reaction (of course, it is legitimate to be upset or not like something; the idea is to let go of the toxicity of the judgments).
3. If anger really is justified, try to describe it without actually using the word "angry." For example, say something like "I really don't like this" or "it really bothers me that _____ is doing that."

4. Practice noticing anger and using it as a signal that you are having a big reaction, and try to identify your alternative, perhaps more primary emotion. Recognize the legitimacy of *that* emotion, and focus your attention on it.

Using Indirect Communication

Communicating indirectly is also a common way to fail to express accurately what you want or feel. There are a couple of different ways that we regularly communicate indirectly. One is we tell the wrong person what we are wanting or feeling. The other is we describe a related phenomenon rather than the thing we really care about, and we assume that the other person knows what we're meaning or wanting.

Everyone knows that direct communication is more accurate and clear. However, lots of things get in the way. For example, we might feel apprehensive that if we tell the person directly, we'll have a fight. So, for couples who fight a lot, being indirect might seem to have some benefits. Of course, being indirect might lessen the chances of an immediate conflict, but it also decreases the chances that your sweetie will understand you or respond to you in the way that you want. So, telling your sister-in-law that you really want to spend more time with your mate (her brother), if communicated at all, likely will not be communicated effectively and could make things worse.

In addition, communicating about one piece of a larger set of thoughts and feelings rarely communicates the most important ones. For example, in the example above, Richard wants more time and more closeness with Ruth. Perhaps one Saturday afternoon, she asks Richard to take care of the kids, so she can do something with her sister. If he is thinking, "Gee, I was hoping to do stuff together today because we haven't spent much time together lately," but instead, he simply says, "I'd rather you stay home," his communication is indirect and murky. Ruth could interpret his denial of her request in any number of ways, many quite negatively. Richard could instead communicate directly, and even negotiate. For example, he might say, "Sure, honey. But I was really also hoping to spend some time together. So, if you go out with your sister for the afternoon, when could we have some time together?" Ruth, now understanding Richard's true goals and desires, is much more likely to try to accommodate him.

Undervaluing Your Wants

Sometimes we become judgmental toward ourselves, which results in feeling vulnerable, humiliated, or ashamed of what we feel or what we want. This is a different kind of unnecessary suffering, because of course we are just who we are, and we want whatever we want and we feel whatever we feel. There are no wrong desires or feelings. It might be inconvenient or troublesome at times (because we can't have what we want, or because what we genuinely feel is painful), but at least it's real. Judging ourselves, saying we should not want what we want or feel what we feel (our primary emotion, that is), is really just denying reality. It's like saying, on a very rainy day when we hoped to do something outdoors, that it just shouldn't be raining or that it is wrong for the clouds to rain. The reality is descriptive, of course: we prefer that it be sunny, we are disappointed that our plans can't be carried out, or maybe we are even demoralized because it rained the last time we made similar plans.

When we want something from our partner but then judge ourselves negatively for wanting it, we really undervalue our own wants and, in effect, undervalue ourselves. Maybe you want your partner to like something (some activity) or someone (a friend) as much as you do, but then you think you are being silly or even ridiculous for wanting that. Or, maybe you just had a lovely long weekend together and miss him or her when you are at work on Monday. But then you think, "How stupid, since we just spent seventy-two straight hours together. I shouldn't miss him/her. Maybe I'm too dependent." Then you feel embarrassed or ashamed and fail to express your love and longing accurately.

It is important to recognize that your wants are justified: there simply is no correct amount of time you should spend together, no amount of love that should be enough (or too much), no amount of attention that is correct and healthy to get from your mate. These are all things that vary from person to person, that vary over time, and must be negotiated from honesty and an acceptance of what you each actually like and want. But this honesty requires a willingness to feel disappointed: as they say, "you can't always get what you want."

Overvaluing Your Wants

There is another phenomenon that interferes with accurate expression: overstating or overvaluing the importance of something (you want or feel), often because you fear that the other person won't take your desires or feelings seriously if you were to state them accurately. This is another example of the long-term cost being significantly greater than the short-term gain. That is, if something is important, it's important for the other person to be able to tell it's important. If *everything* is really important (you communicate them all equally strongly), the other person can't tell which ones are relatively more or less important. And your partner can't respond to everything as though it were life or death. So, in the long run, he or she will simply respond less to everything, making you more frustrated and disappointed. Consequently, it is really more effective to sort out how important something is and express yourself accurately. Again, you also need to be ready for occasional disappointment, not always getting the response you want. At other times, when it's really important, your partner will have the energy to respond in a big way and will be able to tell that this situation is different from most others. In those moments, you will get what you want and be satisfied.

PRACTICE

1. Practice rating how important something is to you before you ask your partner to do it. Maybe use a 0 to 100 scale, in which 0 is not important at all and 100 is the most important thing to come up in the past year.
2. Notice how you express your wants and desires. Can your partner tell from your expression that what you want is low in importance? High?
3. Practice matching the intensity of your expression with the importance of your goals.

Cutting Off Your Nose to Spite Your Face

Finally, there are times that we say things that are clearly the opposite of what we mean or what we want, purely out of bitterness. Maybe you really are tired and are thinking about going to bed early. But you are stewing in judgments and anger, bitter about something that happened earlier. So, when your partner says, in a caring voice, "Honey, you look tired. Maybe you should go to bed early," you respond by saying, "No. I'm not tired. I'm fine." Or, your partner is trying to be nice, maybe following a fight, and offers to do something to help you that would really be nice, and clearly you would like him or her to do it. But you reply, "No thanks. I'm okay."

The problem with these scenarios is not that they create problems in themselves. Rather, the problem is that the opportunity for a repair, for your partner to be able to move closer or do something that you would like, is lost. And, moreover, you are inadvertently telling your partner that she or he cannot read you properly: You seem tired and are tired, but you say you are not. You look like you would like help, and in fact, you want help, but you say you don't. This set of confusing messages could lead a well-intentioned partner, on another occasion, to second-guess what he or she sees: Maybe you really don't need help or really are not tired, even though it seems that way. Consequently, in the future he or she may not bother to offer emotional support or meaningful help in this kind of situation.

Match Your Strategy to Your Goals

Sometimes we know what we want or feel, but we communicate in such a way that our partner cannot respond effectively. For example, Carla had a hectic and frustrating day at work. She came home quite upset and said, "I really hate my job." José, having heard this many times and worrying about Carla, responded in a caring way, telling Carla that they have enough money to get by for a while on José's income, so maybe Carla "should quit her job and look for another, less stressful job." Carla, however, really just wanted José to understand that she'd had a bad day, to be willing to listen to some of the details, to validate her feelings, and to provide some support and soothing. By problem solving, José failed to deliver what Carla really wanted. But, how could José have known this, based on Carla's statement, "I really hate my job"? Carla, already upset, felt misunderstood by José, her emotional arousal peaked, and she quickly started making judgments about José and about herself. This led to a flood of intense, negative secondary emotions. She then started blaming José, "You have no confidence in my abilities. You're always undermining me. This is the best job I've ever had. Just because I had a bad day isn't an excuse to throw it all away. Why can't you just be supportive of me? Does my success threaten you or something?" José, of course, attacked back, and their evening went right down the toilet.

The interaction between Carla and José probably would have gone a lot better if Carla had recognized that she had an *emotional* goal. Then, she could have communicated in a way that would set up José to respond to what she really wanted. Generally, if we have emotional goals, it makes sense to use a strategy that communicates them. Other goals might be *practical,* or *relational.*

Emotional Goals

When we want to feel better, want our partner to understand us, want to receive support, validation, or soothing, we have primarily emotional goals. A great deal of communication in couple relationships actually is intended to achieve something emotional. However, it is very common, especially in distressed relationships, not to express these goals clearly. In relationships that have a lot of conflict, partners often feel vulnerable when they really want soothing or support. The prospect of failing to get desired support only increases those feelings of vulnerability, which makes it hard to ask clearly. Unfortunately, not expressing your goal clearly means it is very unlikely that you will get what you want.

There are two main strategies you can use to get emotional goals met. One is directly clarifying what you want out of the interaction. Above, Carla could have said, "I want to talk about my day, and all I really want is for you to listen and be supportive." The other is describing the situation, focusing on your feelings (Carla also could have said, "When Judy gave Alice the credit for my work, I really felt demoralized and hurt"). Although it may feel awkward or more vulnerable to tell your partner what you want in that moment, it really just makes good sense. When we go to a restaurant, we don't say to the waiter, "I'm hungry." We have to say what we want, or we can't expect to get it very often by chance.

Practical Goals

Sometimes we want something to change, or we want help solving a problem. In these cases, simply being told "I know you are unhappy" is not enough. Perhaps, after months or years of job frustration in which Carla had tried everything to improve her situation on her job, she might conclude that she really wanted to quit and find another job. At that point, if José *only* validated her feelings, saying, "It makes sense that you are so frustrated, given what you have to deal with every day," it would not be enough. Carla, wanting to get a new job but worried about money and her career, might want help problem solving. What salary does she need to bring in so as not to have a big negative effect on their family? Are there adjustments that José and Carla can make in their budget to make it easier for her to quit?

If we want help solving problems, the clearest, most effective thing to do is ask for it. Carla could say, "As you know, I've been doing everything I can to make things better at my job for more than a year. I no longer want to work on tolerating it or trying to make it better. I want to get a new job. But I'm worried about money, how this will affect us. Can we talk about this? I'd really like your help figuring out what to do, how to make this work." This clearly orients José both to what Carla is feeling (he can respond to that, too) and to what she primarily wants from him: help solving the problem. Chapter 10 will address how to go about solving bigger problems, negotiating solutions constructively, and so on.

Relational Goals

Having relational goals, or a desire to improve the relationship, is a bit more complicated. Often, we have a nagging sense of distance from our partner, wanting something more from him or her but not really being able to put our finger on it. Most often, what we really are wanting is more closeness, in one form or another. We might want the other person to understand something, maybe stop doing something or do more of something else in the relationship. But it may not be the "something" that is central but rather an increased sense of understanding, support, or closeness that really is the goal. Both emotional goals and practical goals achieve more closeness in the long run, but relational goals often require a slightly different approach, one that actually combines some of the strategies already discussed.

First, it is important to notice whether a lack of closeness is part of the picture. If it is, then part of the strategy should be to communicate the goal of being closer, getting along better, sharing more, liking each other more, and so on. It's not as likely to be helpful to say *why* you think you are not as close as you would like or have not been getting along, unless you are willing to put the focus on change on yourself. If, in reality, you are thinking or assuming that your partner is implicated in why things are not as you would like, and you try to explain that, it just sounds like you are blaming your partner for it, even if you don't mean to be blaming him or her and truly are not feeling judgmental.

Instead, the strategy should include three parts. It should include a description of your feelings: "Sweetie, I've really been missing having quiet, loving time together, and I'm sad we haven't had much of this for a while. I am not complaining, not at all critical of you: just missing you." It should include a clarification of your goal: "I would really like to be closer, get back to supporting each other more and doing things together, really enjoying each other." Finally, it should include a clear statement asking to work on finding solutions together: "I'd really like us to try some new things, both of us trying to be closer. Can we work on this for a few minutes now and maybe continue later in the week?" Then, you can proceed to collaborate on a solution or at least have a conversation that increases understanding and provides the opportunity for validation. Clearly, when you have a relational goal, it is essential to use a real relational strategy.

PRACTICE

1. For a few days or longer, try to notice what you really want from your partner before you say anything to him or her. Sort out whether you have an emotional goal, a practical goal, or a relational goal.
2. Pick a strategy for expressing yourself that makes it clear to your mate what you are looking for from him or her. Notice if it works and if your increased clarity makes it more likely for your partner to be responsive to your requests.
3. Practice following the steps outlined above, matching your strategy to the type of goal you have.

Effective Expression: The Technical Details

This chapter has covered most of the pieces of the puzzle of how to identify accurately what you want, feel, and so on, and how to set up the situation to communicate these things clearly and effectively. Now, you simply need to put it all together and remember a few nuts-and-bolts issues.

Match Words with Voice Tone, Body Language, and Facial Expression

We communicate a lot with our voice tone, our facial expression, and our body. The more relaxed you are, the more you are able to let go of judgments and blame, the more you are able to find your genuine primary emotions, and the more you are able to let go of anger, the more effortless will be the match between what you say and how you say it. And, the more your words, tone, face, and body are saying the same thing, the more accurate and clear is your communication. The more accurate and clear your communication, the more easily your partner can hear you, can understand you, and can be responsive to what you really feel, think, and want.

Pick a Good Time

Everybody knows that important issues require attention. When you have put all the work into identifying what you want and feel, knowing what your goals are, getting yourself mindful and in a nonblaming, more loving and balanced state or perspective, you really want and deserve your partner's attention. So, it is important not to waste all that effort by picking a time to disclose and express yourself when your partner is not or cannot really pay attention, or when you might have difficulty sustaining your own attention. What are the factors to be aware of? Anything that will likely negatively affect your ability to stay mindful or your partner's ability to become and stay mindful of you.

Have Few or No Distractions

Important conversations cannot work well if kids or other adults are present, someone else wants your attention, the television is on, or one or both people are partially involved in another task (reading the newspaper, on the computer, driving in traffic, in the middle of a busy day at work, cooking dinner, paying bills, or doing chores). Similarly, if one person is about to go somewhere, or someone will likely interrupt you soon, you'll feel a lot of pressure and this increased arousal sets things up to go badly.

Attend to Your Physical Well-Being

Things like being hungry or tired or sick have a big impact on our emotions (especially our reactivity) and our ability to maintain attention. So, it makes sense to practice getting in the habit of saving important conversations (anything involving your feelings or your relationship) for a quiet time when you are both well-fed and not exhausted, and neither of you is in a rush to go somewhere else or do something else. Turn off the television. Put down reading materials. Find a comfortable spot, sit down, take a deep breath, and smile at each other before proceeding.

Jump-Start the Conversation in a Constructive Way

Finally, it is important to remember that this kind of communication is not easy. Your partner may have a flood of emotions, especially fear and anxiety, when you say you want to talk about something, especially if it has to do with your relationship. You may not have had a lot of success engaging in these kinds of conversations in the past. Thus, you wanting to talk not only requires your own skills (all these strategies addressed in this chapter), but also your partner needs a lot of courage and skills. You can make this easier on your partner, and thereby increase the chances of the conversation going well and you getting what you want (understanding, closeness, less conflict and friction, more peace, changes in your interactions, and so on), if you set the tone, or jump-start the conversation in the direction you want it to go.

One way to do this is to clearly communicate that you like your partner. This sounds simple, but it's often as difficult to do as it is effective. Remember that when you are unhappy, in a lot of pain, or want your partner to do something differently, this will be upsetting to your partner. His or her emotions might stay focused on simply caring about you, but easily could become quite negative, reacting to worry thoughts or assumptions, such as "she is mad at me again" or "he doesn't really love me as much as he used to" or "here we go again, another fight, another ruined evening." If you can communicate early that, regardless of what you are going to say, you still love and adore your mate, are still committed to him or her—and even though this is an important thing to talk about it really is not a life-or-death issue—he or she can relax more easily. When arousal comes down (or doesn't go up), your partner is more able to pay attention to you, be less defensive, and more responsive.

For example, Heather and John had fought a lot and were really unhappy in their relationship. So they committed to trying to learn and use the skills in this book. But change is difficult and takes time, and there was a lot of pain still lingering from prior conflict for both of them. Heather did a terrific job preparing to talk with John about her loneliness, how she was really missing him and wanting to spend more time together. She identified her genuine feelings (sadness, loneliness, fear) and what she really wanted (more quiet time together, more conversation about "real" things and not just managing the house and kids, more closeness and intimacy). She let go of blaming John (which had been her previous strategy), and she knew she wanted to find balance in valuing her emotions and desires with valuing John's emotions and desires. She picked a good time to talk and had rehearsed her strategy nicely. But when the time came to ask John to talk, she was overwhelmed with fear ("uh-oh, this isn't going to go well ... I'm just going to make it worse ... but I have to try" played in her head).

Rather than take a few seconds to notice her very reasonable apprehension in this situation, she just kind of grimaced and blurted out, "John, can we talk?" Despite all of Heather's efforts, John simply heard Heather being frustrated with him and anticipated another conversation in which Heather would blame him for a variety of transgressions. He quickly became defensive, did not want to have *that* kind of interaction, and said, "No, I really don't want to talk now," and went upstairs to their bedroom and closed the door. Heather, already on her way toward high arousal, was further triggered by his response, became furious, followed him upstairs, and yelled at him for being "insensitive and not caring" and "not willing to try to save our marriage." You can imagine how it went from there.

However, after more practice, a couple of weeks later, Heather tried it again. She anticipated feeling nervous when it was time to invite John into a conversation and had practiced touching her wedding ring and thinking about how much she loved him. She had taken a few minutes to really notice what she was feeling (missing John) and wanting (more closeness), and had successfully let go of blame, judgments, and anger. So, when she felt that rush of apprehension as she was about to open her mouth, she was able to smile, and her negative emotion did not spike. Her tone was soft, and she was smiling at John when she said, "Honey, I so love our time together. Could we talk for a few minutes about doing a little more of this?" John caught her smile and could not misread her tone. He felt loved rather than anticipating anxiously that he was about to be attacked. He was able to listen, use his own skills, and quite naturally and skillfully responded.

PRACTICE

1. Over the course of many conversations, notice how well your voice tone, intensity, body posture, and facial expression match your words (and the importance of your goals).

2. Think through the situation before you initiate a conversation: "Is this a good time for me, and for my partner? Are there likely to be few distractions? Are we physically ready (not too hungry, tired, wired)?" Proceed only if the timing is right.
3. When you do initiate a conversation, practice starting out in a constructive way, being sure that you communicate that you like your partner before you go on to the substance of what you want to talk about.

Chapter 7

Validating Responses: What to Validate and Why

"Validation" is a word that gets used a lot and has been used by couples therapists and researchers in a variety of ways. This is probably because there are a lot of different ways to validate what someone is doing, saying, thinking, feeling, or wanting. Here, validation is one of two key components of effective communication (along with accurate expression, described in chapter 6). Validating responses have a very different effect than invalidating ones; in close relationships it is clear that we thrive on validation from our spouses and partners while we can barely tolerate being invalidated. Distressed relationships are full of invalidation and low in validation, while happy and successful relationships include heavy doses of validation and little invalidation

(Fruzzetti et al. 2006). Moreover, high levels of invalidation and/or low levels of validation by one partner are associated with higher levels of distress and depression in the other partner (Iverson and Fruzzetti 2006). Being pervasively invalidated is believed to contribute significantly to the development of serious psychological disorders (Fruzzetti, Shenk, and Hoffman 2005; Linehan 1993a). This chapter will explore validation in all its glory: what validation is, and what to validate. Chapter 8 explores different ways to validate and when each is more effective. Chapter 9 will show you how to get yourself to validate things even when you have an urge to be invalidating.

Back to the Couple Two-Step

Chapter 6 focused on the first step in the couple two-step, how you and your partner can express yourselves accurately and clearly. The second step involves responding to that expression in a validating way. Obviously, there are a lot of other options, like ignoring or invalidating each other, but these do not work very well. Validating what your partner is doing, saying, feeling, and wanting is the key to effective communication and is essential to a healthy relationship.

What Is Validation?

Although the term *validation* has been used in a variety of ways, it means something quite specific here. For the purposes of this book, validation between partners is the *communication of understanding and acceptance* (Fruzzetti and Iverson 2004; Linehan 1997). When we respond in a validating way, we communicate that we *understand* a person's experience (emotions, desires, pain, thoughts) or actions and *accept* them (at least in that moment, in that situation). Thus, validation has something in common with empathy (understanding the other person's experience), but it also requires clear communication of that understanding. In addition, a validating response can reflect either an emotional or a more cognitive understanding of your partner's experience (or both). Sometimes, this can be as simple as paying attention and making good eye contact and nodding, or saying "uh-huh" or "right" or "okay." At other times, validating requires a more thorough acknowledgment of the experience, such as "I know you are really disappointed" or "you look really sad."

Perhaps even more important, when we communicate that we understand and accept, we are also implying that the person's experiences or actions make sense, are legitimate, or that they may even be quite normative. Of course we can also directly legitimize by validating in a particular way: "Certainly you feel/think/want X in that situation. Anyone would." It is also possible to communicate that a person's experience is valid, even if we don't yet completely understand it. In these situations, we must gently ask questions, clarifying what we do and do not understand, showing that we are really trying to fully understand and that we assume his or her experience is understandable and legitimate: "Gee, you look tired, like you had a hard day. What happened?"

So, validating communicates understanding of your partner's experience (emotions, wants, goals, opinions) and acceptance of the legitimacy of those experiences. This includes accepting the "facts" about that person's experiences, including accepting his or her descriptions as accurate. Hence, the two-step communication dance, which generally allows a couple to navigate the dance floor of their relationship without too many injuries or stepped-on toes.

What Validation Is Not

Validation is often confused with agreement. Although we certainly can validate by agreeing, it is not necessary. For example, if Henry wants to go out with friends on Saturday night, and Wendy would rather go out alone as a couple, they clearly do not agree. Nevertheless, validating what the other wants is important: Henry can say, "I know you really want us to go out and have a quiet evening alone, that we don't do that as often as you would like." Having validated what Wendy is experiencing, Henry can agree: "So, let's go out together. Maybe next weekend we can go out with Ted and Alice." Or he can disagree: "But, I would really like to see Ted and Alice. We haven't seen them in a long time." Although this latter response might still be conflictual and require further negotiation (or a coin flip), it is off to a more constructive start than if Henry had failed to validate the legitimacy of what Wendy wanted to do, or actually had invalidated her: "You should be satisfied with our alone time. We just went out alone a couple of weeks ago."

In addition, you need to do more than simply repeat back what the other person says, like a parrot. When you do that, you really are failing to understand the other's experience. Understanding is the linchpin.

Finally (and oddly), it is not validating to legitimize something that is not legitimate. For example, if someone holds a mistaken (factually incorrect) belief, it is validating to communicate that you understand that he or she holds that belief, but it would not be validating to agree with or legitimize the mistaken belief itself. And, of course, it is most effective to offer the facts in a nonjudgmental way: "I know you were thinking that the kid's holiday party is Friday after school, but it actually is today."

Why Validation Is Important

Responding with validation to the expression of emotions, wants, opinions, and skillful actions has many important consequences. Validation is a core component of effective communication, soothes frayed emotions, slows negative reactivity (including anger and judgments), facilitates negotiation, builds trust and closeness, and often also enhances self-respect.

Validation Enhances Communication

Responding to your partner's disclosures (accurate expression) with validation completes the communication cycle: one person accurately expresses something, the other listens, understands, and communicates understanding. Or, one person expresses something, the other listens, does not understand, and communicates not understanding, which leads to clarification. Without validation, the person who is expressing might as well be talking to the wall.

In addition, because of the soothing properties of validation, being validated reduces negative emotional arousal, which makes it much easier to express private experiences accurately (figure 5). Thus, validation is a core element in communication. Validation communicates that you are: paying attention; interested in your partner's experience (wants, emotions, thoughts); understanding his or her experience (or at least genuinely trying to understand it); and that you understand (or assume) that his or her experience is legitimate. Validation also communicates that you are *not:* interested primarily in arguing; interested primarily in being right (and in your partner being wrong); responding in a defensive way; responding in an offensive way, trying to be hurtful. It helps the other person express himself or herself accurately, which in turn facilitates your further understanding (and makes future validation that much easier).

When you communicate that you understand and accept your partner's feelings, desires, and so on, most of the time your understanding will be correct, and your partner will feel understood and you can continue communicating. But sometimes, what you understand will not be entirely correct. By also communicating the desire to understand and a willingness to accept the legitimacy of your partner's experience, she or he can simply reexplain any misunderstood parts so that you can complete the two-step successfully, even joyfully (by validating), rather than continuing to talk despite misunderstanding (and dancing into a wall or off a cliff). (Figure 5)

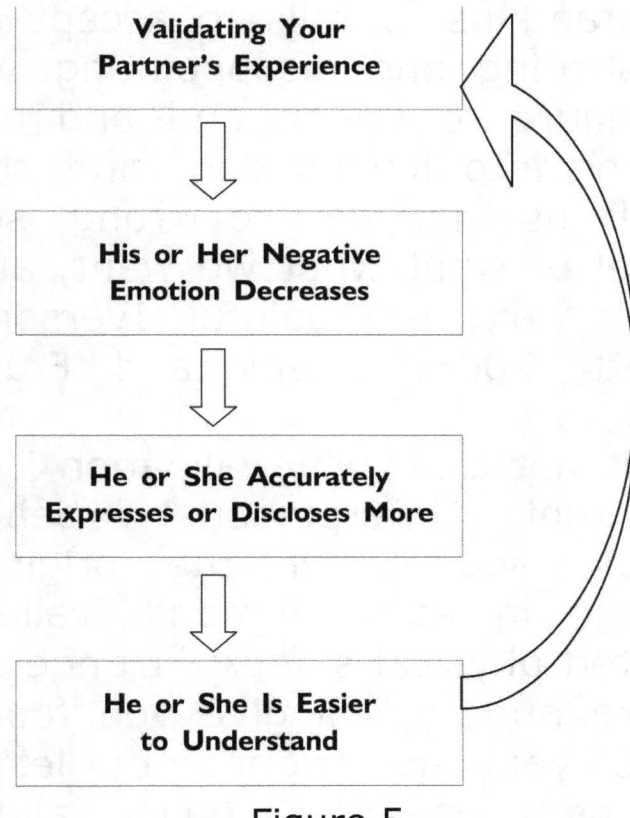

Figure 5

Validation Soothes Emotions

There is something very basic about being understood and accepted. When someone we love, in particular, communicates that she or he understands and accepts what we are thinking, how we are feeling, what we are wanting, we feel relieved, comforted, and soothed. In contrast, when someone we love fails to understand us or fails to accept us, it is frustrating and disappointing. When that failure to understand and accept us turns into invalidation, and she or he tells us that we are wrong, should not feel or want what we want, and so on, it is very, very painful (Iverson and Fruzzetti 2006; Shenk and Fruzzetti 2006).

It is not clear why validation is such a potent interpersonal behavior. Perhaps, soon after the origins of language in early humans, validation predicted physical safety: "I understand you are hungry; I'll give you food" or "I see you are frightened; let's go somewhere safer." Today, validation predicts emotional "safety" and continues to have significant soothing properties. Just imagine a fairly simple situation, one in which you are feeling cold. Somebody else is comfortable and tells you that you *shouldn't* feel cold, that it is plenty warm in the room. What happens to your emotions? You will immediately become emotionally activated. The same thing happens if you are feeling tired, sad, happy, worried, or want or don't want something. When your partner invalidates your experience, you get upset (defensive, attacking, or self-critical). But when your partner understands your experience and accepts you in the moment, you feel soothed and can relax.

Validation Slows (or Turns Around) Negative Reactivity

Because of the soothing properties of validation, it is particularly important to use when a conversation concerns a touchy subject or your emotional arousal already is escalating. If your partner is becoming upset, validating his or her feelings, wants, goals, or opinions will slow down your partner's reactivity, may stop its escalation altogether, or may even transform that arousal into something positive. Of course, when your partner stops escalating negatively, it becomes easier for him or her to validate your feelings, wants, goals, or opinions. Thus, validation by one partner leads to the other validating back, a kind of validation cycle, as shown in figure 6.

Validation Builds Trust and Closeness

Couples who have had a lot of disagreements and regularly have invalidated each other typically develop a virtually instant alert, a kind of hair-trigger sensitivity to even the possibility of the other partner invalidating them. This clearly communicates mistrust that your disclosures and expressions will be valued and understood, that your experience or desires will be accepted. The good news is that with validation, mistrust evaporates and trust builds. In addition, when partners feel understood, valued, and accepted, they naturally feel close to each other. It comforts your partner to know that you know what he or she is experiencing and that you are accepting of him or her. This brings down barriers to closeness and builds those moments of understanding, comfort, and mutuality that are the essence of intimacy. (Figure 6)

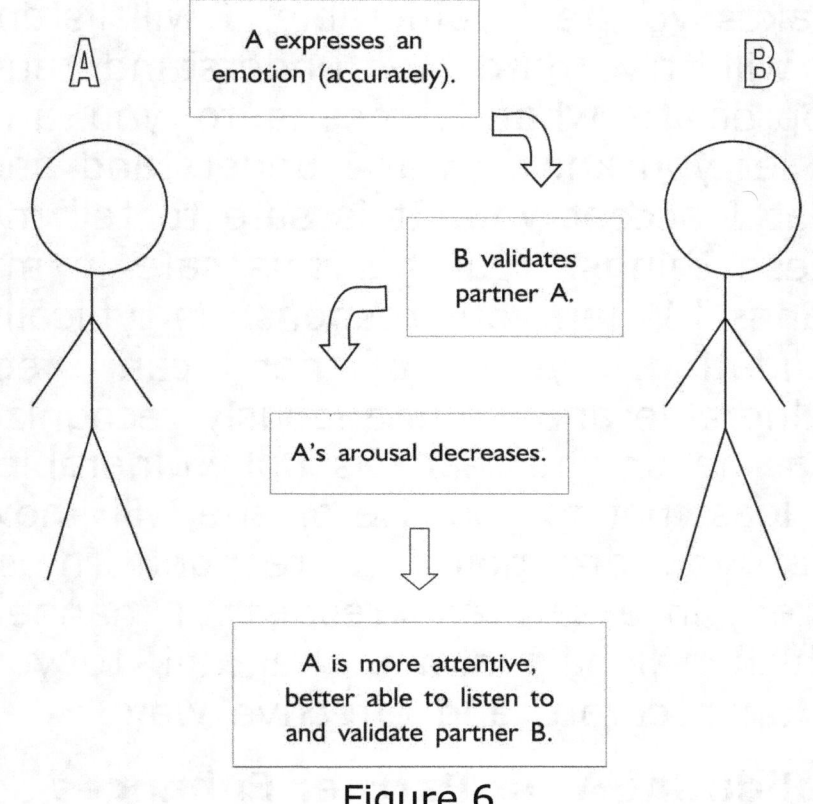

Figure 6

Validation Establishes You as a Safe and Respectful Partner

When you validate, you are clearly responding to what your partner just expressed to you. However, you also are initiating the next round of communication. When you validate, you are inviting your partner to express more, in effect saying, "If you express yourself, if you disclose something that makes you feel vulnerable, I will listen. I will try hard to understand and appreciate what it means to you and to let you know what I understand and that I accept you. It is safe to tell me these things. Your heart is safe in my hands." When your response is typically validating, your partner can feel vulnerable and simultaneously recognize that he or she really is not vulnerable, at least not to you. He or she will know that you are going to respond (most often) in a safe and respectful manner, which will help him or her talk to you in an accurate and effective way.

Validating Your Partner Enhances Your Self-Respect

So far, this chapter has focused on the direct benefits of validation for the person being validated (feeling soothed, increasing his or her ability to express him- or herself accurately) along with some indirect benefits for the person doing the validation (validation reciprocity means that the person validating now will be more likely to be validated in the future). But there is another important benefit associated with validating your partner: doing so increases your own self-respect.

In the middle of an argument, or even when your partner is expressing something that you don't like or don't quite understand, your own negative emotional arousal goes up. As noted, this makes it easy to become judgmental and then to say invalidating things. Then, when your arousal comes back down, you realize that what you said or did was really hurtful, and you regret it. And you likely feel bad about yourself for that behavior: disappointed, guilty, and embarrassed. But, imagine instead of flying off the handle and invalidating the person you love, that you slowed down, let go of judgments, took a minute to bring down your emotional arousal, and tried to be mindful of your partner and your genuine goals. Then you validated your partner.

First, this alternative scenario likely would result in your partner responding very differently, and the whole interaction would probably go better. But, even if it did not improve the outcome of the conversation, imagine how much more self-respect you would have afterwards. Invalidating your partner is really succumbing to being out of control. Alternatively, validating your partner, the person you love, exhibits your skills and your commitment and willingness to do the hard things needed to be a loving partner, which results in considerably more self-respect.

Finding a Valid Target: What Is Valid and How Is It Valid?

Hopefully it is clear how important it is to respond to your partner in a validating way. But what is valid? If we do not necessarily agree with something our partner says, what do we validate? And how? This section explores the different ways that our experiences and behaviors can be valid. Before we can validate anything, we have to find a target that is valid and be able to communicate in what way it is valid.

How Something Can Be Valid

It turns out that there are many different ways that a person's experience or behavior can be valid (Fruzzetti and Iverson 2004; Fruzzetti, Shenk, and Hoffman 2005; Linehan 1997). The main ways are described in the following sections.

It Exists, It Is Real

Although it may seem trivial to say that validating can be as simple as acknowledging that a person's experience is actually real, in fact, this is a very powerful way to validate. And it is a particularly important way to validate when you don't agree with what your partner is saying.

For example, David and Anita argued about a lot of things. If David said he was frustrated or sad, Anita would tell him he shouldn't be, because she had done nothing wrong to cause those negative feelings. Then David would tell Anita that she was wrong to criticize his feelings, and the cycle would continue. In reality, when David said he was sad or frustrated, he was. Or at least he was upset. This was simply true; whether he had misunderstood or overreacted to Anita was irrelevant. Anita felt attacked and blamed, whether David meant to blame her or not, and she believed she had acted fairly, whether David thought so or not. David's communication could benefit from more complete and accurate description, such as "I am really sad we keep disagreeing and fighting. I know this is a problem that *we* have, not just you. I'm not blaming you. I really want us to get better at this." Similarly, Anita's descriptive response could both cool the flames of her escalating defensiveness and make it easier for David to stay nonblaming of her. She might say, "Okay, I can see that our fighting upsets you, makes you sad. It makes me sad, too. I also want us to work this out in a better way. Yeah, there must be things we both can do to make it better." Notice that both partners would simply describe what they hear directly from the other or what they feel themselves.

Being able to simply describe reality (relationship mindfulness) is a really important cornerstone of validation. A flat tire is inconvenient whether it occurs by accident (driving over a nail on the street that fell off a garbage truck), neglect (somebody forgot to sweep the driveway after building something there), or design (someone put a nail under your tire so that it would give you a flat after backing out of your parking space). Of course, the cause of the flat tire (how the nail got there) affects what other emotions you have and what steps, if any, you take to avoid flats in the future. However, it is still inconvenient, and it makes sense that someone would not enjoy the experience.

It is common to hear people (especially counselors or therapists) say things like "feelings are always valid." What this usually means is that if a person feels a certain way, he or she feels that way for a reason. The feelings may be in reaction to faulty data, but the fact is that the person feels what she or he feels, wants what she or he wants, thinks what she or he thinks. It just is what it is.

It Is Reasonable or Legitimate Under Particular Circumstances

Sometimes we can understand how someone feels a certain way, even if that particular reaction is unusual or even not really valid in other ways. For example, some partners have had negative experiences in previous relationships that leave them overreacting or underreacting to their current partners. In these situations, your partner's feelings may be valid (make sense, be legitimate) because of their prior experiences, even though they might not be as legitimate purely in response to the current situation.

Liz was involved with a very aggressive and violent partner, Aaron, for several years. Over this time, she learned to be acutely aware of Aaron's moods. She knew when she was in danger of being verbally attacked or physically assaulted. Eventually, she was able to get out of that abusive relationship, and about a year later, she met Sean, who never had been abusive toward anyone and really was a sweet and mild-mannered guy. When Sean did become upset, however, even about things that had nothing to do with her, Liz immediately felt fearful and would withdraw. Sean was confused and would ask Liz why she was upset with him; he would point out that he had done nothing negative toward her. But this only made Liz more fearful, so Sean simply backed off, accepted Liz's reaction (even though he did not understand it), and tried to reassure Liz of his warm feelings toward her when she later was willing to talk. Over time, Liz realized that she was hypervigilant because of her abusive experiences with Aaron, and that initially when Sean had reminded Liz that he was not upset with her, it had triggered a lot of learned fear from her previous relationship. Aaron had regularly told Liz that she was crazy, that he was not mean or abusive to her. Of course, understanding this helped Sean not take Liz's fear personally, which helped him be validating toward her: "I know you're feeling a little anxious about talking. I'd be happy to talk later or now. Whatever you want."

It's Normative: Anyone Would Think/Feel/Want/Do That

Sometimes the things we think or feel or want or do just make a lot of sense: anyone would do the same. For example, if your partner is late and you don't know where she is, you worry about her. Anyone would. If you love your partner and have not seen him for a few days (maybe he's working out of town), you miss him. Anyone would. If you are unhappy with your job, you might want to get a new job. Who wouldn't? If you applied for a job that would be just perfect, but you didn't get it, you would be disappointed. Anyone would.

People tend to worry that their feelings or desires or actions are not normal. But mostly they are. It is very powerful for you to validate just how normal your partner's feelings are when his or her reactions really are normative.

What to Validate

We have focused a lot on validating emotions—and for good reason. Understanding each other's emotions—and soothing those emotions when they are negative—is an essential part of any close relationship. However, there are a lot of other experiences and behaviors that are valid and that we can validate. This section will cover not only emotions but many other experiences and behaviors that are important to all of us and for which awareness (mindfulness), acceptance (being nonjudgmental, not rejecting your partner's experience as invalid), and validation (communicating your understanding about the legitimacy of his or her experience) are essential responses in a close relationship.

Emotions

When you understand your partner's emotions, you can respond in a variety of validating ways. This is true whether those emotions are incidental or intense, enjoyable or painful. Validating painful emotions soothes them, and validating enjoyable emotions enhances your partner's pleasure. In both cases, you are jumping in and sharing the experience a little bit. This enhances your understanding and acceptance of your partner's experience, thus bringing you closer, and it cements your bond with each other so that your partner is better able and more willing to understand and accept you. Emotions are an important part of who we are. Validating emotions allows you to share your lives with each other.

Wants or Desires

Everyone goes through life with things we would prefer to do or to happen. Some of these are quite important, others more incidental. Regardless, knowing your partner's wants in life (big and small) helps you to know him or her in important ways. What would she do if money were not an issue? What would he do if he had more free time? What are your partner's real goals: What does he or she want from life? How about from next weekend? If you validate your partner's wants or goals, you will likely find that your partner will tell you more. If you fail to validate or invalidate them, you may find yourself shut out from these important pieces of your partner's life.

Knowing his or her desires also allows you to respond in ways that are validating: you can facilitate your partner getting what she or he wants (a special kind of validation), or soothe your partner when you realize that she or he did not get what was desired. Validating your partner's wants also helps him or her decide whether to keep putting energy into trying to get something or to let it go and start taking steps to move on.

Beliefs and Opinions

Everyone has opinions, and many of these are very tightly held beliefs. To some extent, our beliefs are part of who we are, just like our emotions and our desires. When someone understands us, accepts our thoughts or beliefs, we can relax in the world. In some ways, that is why we join clubs or organizations and enjoy hanging around with people who like the same things we do. However, opinions and beliefs can be controversial, and often the more controversial ones are those that we feel most defensive about. That is why it is important to validate what your mate thinks, what his or her opinions are, even if you have different ones. By being validating, you communicate that the other person has a right to her or his opinions, that they are legitimate. Then, even if you disagree, you do so from a position of respect, obviating any need for your partner to become defensive.

Actions

It is important to validate what your partner actually does. This might include noticing his or her efforts at work, with chores, or actions and activities with children. It also includes doing nice things for your partner without strings attached (see chapter 5). In addition, it is important that you notice, appreciate, and acknowledge any activities or actions that are important to your mate. Inquiries like "I noticed you cheering for the Red Sox. Who won the game?" or "Was that your mom on the phone? How are things?"

communicate your interest in your partner, appreciation of his or her interest in something, and acceptance (you are content with what he or she is doing, not trying to change it). In other situations, when you offer a thank you in response to your partner's behavior, you are acknowledging your partner's actions and simultaneously disclosing your appreciation. Everyone enjoys being noticed and appreciated by loved ones.

Suffering

The world is full of suffering of all types, and all of us suffer at times. Having someone close to us during times of suffering acts as a balm. Validating suffering communicates caring, understanding, acceptance, and a willingness to share a little of that suffering. Nothing is more soothing than to have your partner with you, accepting your pain, understanding your experience, and sharing it with you.

PRACTICE

1. Think about what your mate was feeling the last time you had a

conversation. Did it make sense? In what ways were his or her feelings legitimate?

2. Recall the last time you were upset with your partner. Try to let your judgments go and see if you can find a way to understand what he or she was wanting or feeling. Clearly, your partner is not crazy, so whatever she or he felt was legitimate in some way or other. How?

3. Practice noticing what your partner is wanting, thinking, feeling, and doing (including being happy or feeling a lot of suffering). Try to assume that his or her experience or behavior is legitimate in some way (it is). Can you notice how his or her experience is legitimate? You don't need to say anything yet; just practice noticing.

4. Try to understand something about your partner's expression or behavior in a previous situation (weeks or months ago) that you had a hard time understanding at the time. Can you now find ways in which those experiences or

behaviors were valid or made sense?

5. When you are upset with your partner, notice how your own strong emotions or your own judgments get in the way of seeing the validity in your partner's experiences or behaviors. Try some of the earlier skills in the book to reduce your emotional arousal and to let go of judgments. Is it easier to understand your partner's feelings/desires/thoughts/actions?

Chapter 8

Validating Responses: How to Validate Your Partner

Now that we have discussed why it is important to respond to your partner with validation, and you know *what* to validate (targets), it is time to spell out how to do it. This chapter will explain a whole variety of ways to validate whatever your partner is feeling, wanting, doing, etc., both verbally and with your actions (Fruzzetti 1995, 1997; Fruzzetti and Iverson 2004, 2006; Linehan 1997).

We will begin by identifying several different ways to validate verbally. In addition, however, there are many ways to validate without words. This turns out to be a good thing when you can't think of what to say, of course, but it is also important in other ways.

Verbal Validation

Chapter 7 identified some basic ways that anyone's experiences or behaviors can be valid. This section will discuss what to say or do to communicate verbally or in conversation that you understand and accept what your partner is experiencing or doing. Although they are discussed separately, sometimes a validating response will include elements of several of these ways to validate at one time.

Show That You Are Paying Attention and Listening Actively

When you are mindful of your mate, you are open to what she or he is experiencing, less defensive, more able to simply notice it. When you are communicating that you are paying attention, listening actively and openly, you are validating in an important way. This counts as verbal validation, since it occurs during dialogue, even though this particular way of validating does not require you to say anything. This kind of validation demonstrates that your partner is important to you and that you are open to understanding. There really are two parts here: becoming mindful of your partner, really paying attention, not becoming judgmental or defensive, and staying open to what she or he expresses; and communicating gently that you are interested, attentive, and listening actively with an open mind, accepting of what she or he is saying or doing.

The simplest ways to show this nonjudgmental active listening are to drop your other activities (put down reading, turn off the TV or stereo); relax your body and facial muscles; look at your partner, including good eye contact, which communicates that you are willing to listen with your full attention; respond naturally in small ways that show her or him that you are following (nodding your head, giving ordinary conversational cues that show you are tracking and understanding, such as "um-hmm" or "right").

Sometimes, this first kind of validation is sufficient: you demonstrate your interest and openness, and your partner feels heard and understood, and that's all that's needed. However, at other times more may be required. Even if more words are required to respond in a validating way, this first level is virtually always an essential component of validation.

PRACTICE

1. Practice this type of validation with anyone. Notice your posture, muscle tension, and whether you are feeling open to what your partner has to say and that you are also showing that openness clearly. Make good eye contact and be sure that the other person can tell that you are interested and that she or he has your undivided and nonjudgmental attention.
2. Practice this with your partner. After a while, check in to see if she or he feels that you are genuinely interested and paying attention. Make adjustments to how you communicate your attention in

response to whatever your partner tells you. Continue practicing.

Acknowledge Your Partner's Experience

Sometimes it is important just to acknowledge what the other person is doing, saying, feeling, thinking, or wanting. As noted in chapter 7, this is particularly important when you are not entirely in agreement. For example, if David feels lonely and is thinking this is because he and Anita have not been getting along well, he might simply say, "You know, Anita, I've been feeling lonely." Under these circumstances, it might be easy for Anita to simply say, "Yeah, you seem sad," which communicates to David that she understands and accepts his feelings. But maybe David feels that the reason they have not been getting along well is Anita's fault, and he blames her, saying "I'm really feeling alone. You're always criticizing me, and I'm tired of it." Anita might be tempted to say, "Hey, it takes two to tango," but that would fail to validate the completely valid part of David's expression, and instead would likely lead to escalating conflict and more negative emotion and distance. Anita could simply say, "Yeah, you seem sad," just as in the first example. By acknowledging the incontrovertibly legitimate part of what David is saying, Anita communicates at least a partial acceptance of his feelings and further communicates her openness to listening and understanding. It does not mean that she agrees that it is her fault; that discussion may not be fruitful at all. Rather, she communicates that she sees David's sadness, his loneliness, and is willing to accept it and be with him at that moment. Chances are good that this will slow David's reaction down, and he may even be able to let his judgments go and become more descriptive, perhaps responding to Anita, "Hmm. You seem sad, too. I guess not getting along is crappy for you, too."

Acknowledging the reality of what your partner is experiencing is potent. Not only are you understanding and accepting, and communicating that understanding and acceptance, but you are *not* providing the typical, problematic response of high-conflict couples: you are *not* invalidating or criticizing and hence *not* escalating the conflict. In fact, you are deescalating it.

Sometimes you can simply acknowledge what your partner is saying, but sometimes your partner expresses things nonverbally or behaviorally. You can acknowledge what he or she is expressing in these ways, too. If she has a sad expression, you can say, "You seem sad." If he keeps trying to find a store that has a particular present for your child or other family member, you can say, "You really want to get that for her, don't you!"

The reality is that, like all forms of validation, this is easy to do when you are content and not emotionally negatively aroused but very difficult to do when you get angry and judgmental, or have a lot of fear or a lot of pain. Therefore it is important to practice this skill a lot, including rehearsing it in your mind, so that the simple words come to you automatically when you need them.

PRACTICE

1. Practice this type of validation with anyone, starting in situations in which you are not upset. Notice the natural ways that you do this, and write down three or four typical things you might say and the way you say them.
2. Practice this validation skill with your partner, whenever it seems appropriate and you can get yourself to do it. Notice how she or he responds.
3. Recall recent conflict situations with your partner or spouse. See if any of the kinds of validating statements you came up with in step 1 might have been effective in stopping the conflict from getting worse. In your head, practice saying them over and over in those situations.
4. Identify what you could do to bring your emotion down enough to be able to actually provide these kinds of validating statements in difficult situations. Consider the skills from earlier chapters and build them into

a plan for how to be more validating of your partner in tough situations.
5. Implement your plan! Even in difficult situations, try to validate what your partner is feeling or wanting, saying something like "I know you feel _____" or "I can tell that you want _____," but of course use your own words and your best soft, genuine, loving (mindful) style.

Ask Questions to Clarify Your Understanding

Sometimes we think we understand what our partner is experiencing, but we're not sure, or the way we understand something seems a little different from what our partner says. When these situations occur, asking questions to clarify (as opposed to prove your partner wrong) can be a very helpful part of validation.

In the simplest situations, just notice that you don't understand something about what your partner is expressing. In a gentle way, describe what you do and do not understand, and ask for clarification. Remember that when a couple has a long pattern of conflict, questions can easily come across as challenges, so be very careful not to question the legitimacy of what the person is saying or experiencing. Rather, communicate that you are interested and accepting but that you just don't completely understand and really do want to understand.

Miranda seemed really upset after getting off the phone, so Alex asked her what had happened. Miranda told him that she was upset that her parents had decided not to visit the following month as planned. Alex was confused, for he knew that Miranda had wanted to postpone her parent's visit until later because of all the other activities and commitments they already had for that week. So, he said to her gently (standing close, relaxed, looking directly at her), "Miranda, you seem really upset and disappointed. But I'm confused because I thought you wanted your parents to visit later. So, I'm not understanding something. Why are you disappointed?" With this acknowledgment and clarifying question, Miranda then was able to respond, "Well, you're right, I did want them to postpone. But they were really hurt by my asking them to change the dates, and they didn't understand that it was only *that* week that was a problem, that I really do want them to come. And now they say they'll just wait until Thanksgiving to visit. That's not what I wanted to happen!" Now, Alex understood and was able to validate completely Miranda's feelings, provide support and encouragement, and later even help think of ways to get her parents to change their minds.

In other situations, confusion may arise because a person is feeling more than one thing, and so expression of those feelings needs to be disentangled. Alternatively, something seems missing, not expressed, which one partner really thinks the other is experiencing. For example, when Eric came home, he slammed the door and stomped around the house. Hannah said to him, "Eric, you seem upset. What's wrong?" Eric then told her that the project he had been working on for weeks, the one thing at his job that he was really excited about, had been cancelled. He said, "I can't believe it. Why did they let me put so much work into it if they were just going to can it now? It really pisses me off." Hannah could see that Eric was, indeed, angry. But she also knew from many previous conversations that Eric was really excited about the project and had hoped that he would get to play an important role in it. Knowing Eric's prior feelings about this made her wonder if maybe he was also really disappointed, not just angry. She soothed him physically by rubbing his shoulder and sitting close to him, and then validated him in a variety of ways, including asking him about disappointment. "Oh, Honey, this is terrible news! Of course you're upset, who wouldn't be? Given how much you were hoping this project would work out, I'd imagine you would be really disappointed, too. Are you disappointed?" Eric felt a little bit of comfort from Hannah, even though he was still upset about the project. Hannah's touch, gentle voice tone, reassurance, and openness to validating and supporting him made him feel a little better. As his arousal came down, he realized that he was, in fact, very disappointed. He had missed noticing his disappointment in the midst of his frustration, and it got further lost when he became judgmental about his boss. Although feeling disappointed was hard, the feeling was genuine, and identifying that emotion and talking about it a little bit helped.

Notice how Hannah was able to identify Eric's disappointment even before he did. This is common in couples because partners know each other well and because our own emotional response to something that happens to our partner is smaller than our partner's own response. With fewer judgments and less emotional arousal, we can see more clearly. Notice also that even though Hannah was fairly sure she knew what Eric was feeling (and she turned out to be correct), she did not tell Eric what he was feeling. That would have been invalidating, because first, his disappointment was "hidden" behind his high arousal and judgments, so he was not actually quite experiencing it yet, and second, if she had been wrong, Eric would have felt terribly misunderstood and distant from Hannah. It was really important for her to support him at this time, not to create distance.

PRACTICE

1. Practice asking clarifying questions any time you are not sure you understand what your partner is saying, wanting, or feeling. Be sure to do this in a nonthreatening way that communicates clearly that you want to understand. Notice your tension, position, facial expression, and voice tone. Be sure to take a moment to be mindful of your partner before you say anything.
2. Talk with each other about the best ways to ask each other for clarification. Try to do what your partner tells you is most reassuring, does not trigger defensiveness, and most helps him or her know how to clarify.

Understand Partner Problems or "Mistakes" in a Larger Context

When one of you has made a mess of something, made a major mistake or blunder, or done something harmful or dysfunctional, emotions on everyone's part are likely to run high. Consequently, validation in this situation can be as difficult as it is important.

First, remember to validate your partner's feelings, wants, and so on even if those experiences have led in some way to problematic behaviors or follow from problematic behaviors. For example, feeling miserable makes sense in a lot of situations, but even extreme misery doesn't mean that harmful behaviors (toward yourself or toward others) are a legitimate way to handle those situations. So, maybe one of you has done something impulsive and/or dangerous or irresponsible and caused harm (drove the car after drinking, smashed something, overdosed on medication, failed to go to work and didn't call in sick). The idea is that the problematic or dysfunctional behavior may not be something to validate (except to acknowledge that it happened) but that the things that led up to the behavior can certainly be understood, as can the consequences.

The idea here is to keep the big picture in mind even when you or your partner does something very problematic. We are not only our most recent gaffe, not only our worst behavior; we have other, more positive and successful behaviors in our repertoires and are complete human beings. So, the first step is to remember this larger context. This is the person you love. He or she has many qualities that are likable and lovable. The next step is to understand that we do even dysfunctional things for reasons. This is not to excuse dysfunctional or hurtful things, but being nonjudgmental can lead us to accept the reality of the situation and move on.

Even in these situations, it may be important to validate what is valid about your partner's experience. Typically, this means validating feelings and desires.

Perhaps your partner has been miserable at work and impulsively quit today, and this plunges the family into financial peril. You can understand how miserable a person must be to quit a job this way. That does not mean you have to agree with the action or like it. And, of course, it is important to express accurately (and nonjudgmentally) your reactions to the situation.

Thus, when your partner is doing something problematic or even dysfunctional, it is important to validate what is valid about it, but it is also important not to validate what is invalid about it. For example, if your partner has had a really difficult day, he or she might be quite tired, overwhelmed, have a lot of feelings, and be in a lot of emotional pain. These experiences make sense, and validating them likely would help. She or he might have urges to drink or use drugs to cut off or escape from the negative emotions. Although it might make sense (be valid) to have these urges, drinking or drug use would not be "valid" ways to manage negative emotions.

Wendy longed to spend more time with Henry and often asked him to be more attentive to her. But Henry was invalidating of Wendy: "You shouldn't want to spend so much time together. You're just too clingy and needy." Wendy became flooded with negative emotion. She felt ashamed and added to it by self-invalidating: "Maybe Henry's right, I'm too needy; I must be an awful wife for him, and he deserves better." This led her to hopelessness and even thoughts of suicide. It would be important for Henry (and anyone interacting with Wendy) to validate her feelings (that she is, in fact, feeling fearful, disappointed, overwhelmed, hopeless, and/or shame) and to acknowledge that those feelings make a lot of sense: Henry rarely spent as much time with her as she would like, so it made sense to feel one-down. Similarly, when someone (in this case her partner, Henry) is that critical and invalidating, it is pretty normal to feel bad about yourself and ashamed. In addition, it is important to recognize and to validate the fact that she had suicidal thoughts or urges ("I know you are having suicidal thoughts"). But it would be important not to validate suicide (or drinking, drug use, aggression, or violence) as legitimate options. Thus, feelings can be valid given certain situations or problems. However, some "solutions" to those problems may not be really valid; that is, they may actually make the person's life, situations, or relationship worse in the long run.

Finally, it is not validating to legitimize a person's judgments, whether the judgments are about themselves or others, or any behavior that degrades someone or treats someone as incompetent or unworthy. This can be complicated. For example, sometimes one partner will express a lot of criticism or even contempt for herself or himself ("I'm such a screwup"). If the other partner is angry and likely judgmental, it may be easy to agree with the first partner, but this just further invalidates him or her. It would be more accurate and validating at the same time to respond by describing your own nonjudgmental thoughts about the specific situation ("well, I wish you hadn't done that, it does make the situation harder to solve").

Alternatively, sometimes one partner might be very judgmental of another person (like a boss or neighbor). It might be tempting to jump on the judgmental bandwagon and pile on further judgments. However, it is far more validating in the long run to find an accurate experience (emotion, desire) to validate ("it makes sense that you're upset with her" or "of course, you'd really rather not have to work with her again tomorrow") than to agree with the judgmental partner ("yeah, she's a real piece of work"). Ultimately, using good sense and keeping your values in mind will help you know what, and how, to validate.

PRACTICE

1. Think about something problematic or dysfunctional that you have done (recently, or even a long time ago). What led up to your behavior? Were your feelings valid? How were they valid? What were your feelings afterwards? What would have been

helpful for a loving partner to say to you, without suggesting that the problem behavior was okay?
2. Talk with your partner about how to handle such situations for each of you. What would be constructive? How can you validate the valid parts without supporting the problematic or dysfunctional parts?
3. Pick a situation from a while back, one that is no longer fresh and does not immediately get your emotions up. Try to talk through the episode, validating the valid parts, keeping the big picture of your partner in mind.
4. When your partner is self-critical, try to validate the underlying emotion and ignore the judgment. Try the same thing when your partner is judgmental about someone else. Remember that you will both feel better, more consistent with your values, if you stay descriptive; stick to what the person did, how you reacted, what you like and don't like, want and don't want.

Understand Historical Reasons for Current Experiences

It's important to focus on how your partner's reactions (whether they are problematic or not) make sense, given his or her previous experience. There was an example of this in chapter 7, where Liz reacted with fear toward her partner Sean even though he was not doing anything threatening and had never done anything like that. She reacted this way because of her experience with a previous abusive partner. Her fear made sense because of her earlier experience.

Many of our reactions are learned. For example, if people around us are consistent, decent, and honest, we generally learn to trust people. If instead, people around us are frequently dishonest, inconsistent, or willing to take advantage of us, we learn to be more cautious. The trouble is that it is often extremely difficult to pinpoint how a person learned to respond a particular way. Usually, validating means assuming the best and giving our partner the benefit of the doubt. If she is reacting in a way that doesn't make sense, assume that if you understood enough about her previous experiences, her reactions would make sense. If his behavior is enigmatic, there probably are understandable reasons for it that you just don't know.

When a relationship is going well, it can be helpful to learn about what your partner's life was like before, both in his or her family of origin and in previous romantic relationships. The idea is not to be a voyeur, but rather to understand a bit more about your partner. Doing so will hopefully help you give your partner the benefit of the doubt when you are confused about his or her reaction.

However, knowing that there are valid explanations for a person's actions and reactions does not mean ignoring the current circumstances. You should always ask clarifying questions to find any current factors that may have influenced your partner's response.

PRACTICE

1. Talk with your partner. Each of you can pick one thing from your early family life or from a previous romantic relationship that you think has had a big influence on your reactions to your partner. Discuss these. As you talk, be sure to validate in terms of previous experiences: "It makes sense that you worry that I might react that way now that I know how she/he reacted."
2. After validating, you can also clarify your own reactions via accurate disclosure and expression: "But I hope you can notice as we are talking that I don't feel that way at all."

Find the "Of Course" in His or Her Experience

In many, many situations, our reactions just make sense. They are quite typical. Almost anybody would react similarly. When this is the case, validating that our partner's feelings or desires or actions are normative is just what is needed. In situations of loss, or when we don't get what we want, people feel sad or disappointed. When we don't spend much time with our partner, we miss him or her. When bad things happen that are beyond our control, we feel frustrated. When we get what we want, we feel happy or satisfied.

Finding the "of course" means that you see that, of course, your partner would feel that way or want that or do that. Just about anybody would. It makes perfect sense! The trick is to be able to stand back and look at the situation from a normative perspective. If the situation does not involve you, this usually is easier. If your mother-in-law has a life-threatening illness, of course your partner is both sad and worried about her. If your partner gets a much-desired promotion, of course he or she is excited and happy. However, what about when you are arguing and you say something mean? Well, in the abstract, it is easy to see how, of course, he or she is hurt. But in the heat of the moment, you may be full of judgments and actually blame your partner: "If she/he didn't criticize me, then I wouldn't have said that."

Imagine what would happen if, instead, you validated the hurt. What if you simply said, "You know, of course you feel hurt. What I said was really mean." Interestingly, this often will bring about the end of the escalation. There is still a repair to be made but you must stop the destructive interaction before any repair is possible. We will discuss the tough situations in which this kind of validation is required more in chapter 9. However, you can now practice this kind of validation in less charged situations.

PRACTICE

1. Notice that your partner actually responds to a lot of things in ways that most people would respond. Become aware of this by practicing a quick analysis several times each day: "She feels _____. Is that how the average person might feel in this situation?" Or, "He wants

_____. Would most people want that right now?" Just notice and be aware.
2. In situations that don't involve you, practice validating in this way. Simply say, "Of course, you feel/want/did that. Anybody would do the same." Or, use your own words that convey how completely normative and reasonable her or his reaction or action was.
3. Now try validating even when your partner's reaction concerns you. Start by choosing something that happened a few days or weeks ago, something about which you are not still raw. Practice what you are going to say ahead of time, so you don't have to come up with words in the moment (if your emotions go up, it might be hard to find the right words), and then validate your partner's experience or behavior.
4. Now, try validating this way in current situations, as they unfold. Step back, notice if his or her reaction really is what most people would do. If so, say so. Notice how

this validation affects the course of your interactions.

Allow Yourself to Be as Vulnerable as Your Partner: "Me, Too"

Imagine that when you were starting to date your partner, at the end of the first date, she or he had told you, "I had a really good time. I hope we can get together again next weekend." What if you had responded, "I can see you had a good time" or "I am confused. What made it enjoyable for you?" or "I know. Everybody has a good time with me on a date like this." That would have been the end of the relationship. The ways of validating that we have discussed so far just don't fit the situation. The reason in this example is that the person has made herself or himself vulnerable to you, leaving herself or himself hanging out on a limb. What is required is that you show similar or reciprocal vulnerability. In this situation, if you wanted to be validating (and wanted another date), you would say something like, "I had a good time, too" or "I'd like to get together again, too." Or, you would simply say, "me, too."

When everything's going well, it's easy to validate with "me, too." But, sometimes one partner will be quite emotionally vulnerable to the other, even though things have not been going well and negative emotions are all around. For example, Jasmine and Jared had been alternating between fighting with each other and avoiding each other, not really able to get unstuck for some time. Each was on hair-trigger alert and reacted defensively at any perceived signs of criticism or invalidation. However, Jared practiced his mindfulness skills and realized that he missed Jasmine and really wanted to try to be closer, to try to let some of the past go. After dinner one night, he said to Jasmine, "I have been thinking about how long it has been since we were really close, and I've been feeling really sad about it. I miss you so much. I want to do better. I want us to do better. I want to be close to you; I love you so much."

In a situation like this, in which one partner is open and vulnerable, it is simply not validating to acknowledge that vulnerability ("I can tell you are sad") or even to say how "anybody would feel that way." Instead, to be validating, you have to be vulnerable also. Jasmine had started out by feeling a lot fear and becoming tense in her shoulders and back. As she listened to Jared, she tried to relax her muscles, to just notice him and be in that moment, observing and ignoring the flood of thoughts and judgments that started to cascade through her mind. As she listened actively and nonjudgmentally, she noticed that she felt a huge rush of sadness, and she felt her affection for Jared, which had been blocked out by the fog of mistrust and anger that had permeated their relationship lately. She responded, "I miss you so much, too." Jared relaxed further, and they were able to hold each other and start the process of reconnecting, letting blame and judgments fall away and replacing them with mindful awareness of their own commitment and love for each other.

In its essence, this reciprocal vulnerability can be summarized by two words: "me, too." That is, "I am just as invested in you as you are in me, just as much devoted to you as you are to me, want things to go well as much as you do, am disappointed in our problems just as you are," and so on. Simply saying, "me too" is often all that is required in these situations. In fact, when we are genuinely and lovingly aware of our partner's vulnerabilities, we often feel a lot of emotions (usually love, connection, compassion), so it may be hard to say much more. Fortunately, this is all that is required in most situations, at least to start down a constructive path.

PRACTICE

1. Practice noticing when your partner is vulnerable to you. It might be with words, but it could also be with other forms of communication, like taking your hand, touching you sweetly, or making warm eye contact. Be mindful of his or her vulnerability, and try to relax and

notice whether you, in fact, want some of the same things (a good relationship, less arguing, more closeness).
2. Rehearse in your mind getting yourself willing to be vulnerable too. Just imagine being able to say "me, too" in some of these situations. Does it feel genuine? What do you need to do, what skills do you need to practice, to be able to actually be vulnerable in those moments with your partner? Whatever is needed, practice that.
3. Now, let down your guard and reciprocate: match his or her tone, actions, and vulnerability, and say (in words or actions), "me too."

Respond with Your Actions in a Validating Way

Finally, there are times when you can respond in a validating way without using words. Some situations don't require a lot of talking but instead require taking action. For example, if you notice that your partner is taking a nap on the sofa and seems cold (maybe she is shivering a little), you wouldn't wake her up to say, "Oh, honey, I can see that you are cold," just as you wouldn't say, "It is only 62 degrees in here! Anybody would be cold." Of course, these would be most unhelpful (and quite silly). Instead, put a blanket on her or turn up the heat or snuggle next to her and share your body warmth. These responses convey your understanding and acceptance of her experience in a far more important way than talking about how legitimate it is to be cold.

Just as with other types of validating responses, it is easier to take validating action when negative emotions are not high. But, in highconflict couples, partners can get in the habit of a kind of knee-jerk disagreement, which must be overcome. For example, your spouse or partner might come home, looking exhausted, and tell you what a difficult day it has been. Maybe it was his turn to make dinner. The obvious thing to do is to consider leftovers, a quick and easy meal, or take-out. But, if there has been a lot of conflict, you might start making it complicated: "It's not fair that he should get out of making dinner. He wouldn't support me if the situation were reversed." These are judgments that interfere with responding in a decent and validating way.

In order to respond with action in a validating way, you need to do three things: stick with the facts (notice what she or he really needs right now, what would work); stay mindful (nonjudgmental) and don't fall into the cesspool of judgments and righteousness; and find a way to respond that does not compromise your self-respect but does meet his or her present need.

Just the Facts

Identifying facts is easy when you are objective, hard when you are highly emotional. What are the facts? Be descriptive. If she says she is tired, believe her. If he says he is hungry, believe him. If she says she wants to go out to dinner, believe her. If he says he hates his job, believe him. But note that the facts do not dictate how you must respond.

Identify What Is Needed

If your partner is tired, are there ways to relieve her burden? Can you respond in some way that helps (regardless of whether she specifically asks for you to respond)? What would help? If he is hungry, you could feed him or let him know where the food is. Both show (if you are sincere) your caring and acceptance. If she wants to go out to dinner, is that okay? Can you afford it? Do you have the time? Energy? If so, go. But if not, you are not necessarily invalidating her experience. You can say, "I know you want to go, but I am worried about our finances," and negotiate from there.

Respond Effectively, Maintaining Your Self-Respect

The bottom line is, if you can respond to what your partner is expressing (whether it is a verbal request or simply an expression of a feeling or a desire), and doing so does no harm to you, then do it. But if you feel genuinely uncomfortable with a particular response, either find another active way to respond or stick with verbal validation.

For example, Sara was really tired after a long day. She and Matt had an agreement that when one person cooked dinner the other person did the dishes. Matt cooked dinner, so it was Sara's turn for dish duty. She was obviously tired and said, "I really am exhausted and don't feel like doing the dishes." In this situation, Matt immediately believed that Sara was tired. He wondered, though, if she was trying to get him to do the dishes. After letting his judgments go ("she shouldn't try to slough this off on me") he realized that he (or anybody else), when really tired, might try to get somebody else to do one of his chores for him. Then he considered doing the dishes. Clearly, Sara would appreciate it, and Matt was not particularly tired. Volunteering to do the dishes would be very validating of her exhaustion. In most situations, doing the dishes would be a very validating thing to do.

But, it is not *required.* That is, if Matt noticed that this situation comes up a lot and honestly thinks Sara is unfair (he does her chores a lot, she rarely does his), maybe he should stick with verbal validation: "Yes, Sara, you look really tired. What happened to make you so exhausted?" Then, he could listen to her talk about her day, perhaps even while she does the dishes. This kind of verbal validation would be useful, even if doing the dishes for her might also be helpful in a different way.

This can become even more complicated when one partner asks the other to do something. Clearly, it is validating to do what is asked. Whenever it is possible and it would be constructive (without sacrificing self-respect), go ahead and do what's asked. But, the only *fact* is that she or he *wants* you to do something. If you cannot do the task, obviously you will not. If you do not want to do it, that's okay *if* your reasons are nonjudgmental (not full of "shoulds" or "shouldn'ts"). Either way, if you don't do what is asked, it will still be very helpful to validate what is valid: your partner wants validation from you and will be disappointed if you don't give it. Just because you don't want to or cannot do something does not mean that your partner should not want you to.

For example, Ginger really loved to dance, but Fred did not usually want to go. Fred sometimes thought that, because he wasn't much of a dancer, Ginger should not ask him to go dancing, maybe should stop even wanting to go. It turned out that when Fred validated Ginger's desires and enjoyment of dancing ("honey, I know you would love to go, but I just have two left feet, so it's not much fun for me"), Ginger felt okay about not going. Fred could further validate Ginger's disappointment, even though she might not have clearly expressed it ("and I'm guessing this is disappointing, because I almost never want to go"). And, he could be responsive also by suggesting alternatives: "Maybe we can do something else together that's active and fun."

Finally, it is often important to communicate your nonjudgmental reasons for not doing what is asked of you. Otherwise, it will be easy for your partner to simply see you as unwilling, unhelpful, or critical. Use your mindfulness skills and describe your thoughts and feelings accurately, ideally in a steady and loving tone (neither defensive nor critical), and be sure to validate your partner's disappointment.

PRACTICE

1. Practice being responsive to your partner in nonconflict situations. If she or he is frustrated, offer to help. If distressed, provide some comfort. Share the burden; share the joys.
2. Evaluate some recent situations in which you might have been more actively responsive to your partner. What got in the way? Did you make a balanced decision or a reactive one? If it was unbalanced, figure out which skills you need (mindfulness, letting go of judgments, awareness of your partner) to be more balanced next time. Practice those skills.

3. When you choose not to be responsive, practice verbal validation, making sure to validate your partner's disappointment.
4. Practice being actively responsive whenever you can.

Chapter 9

Recovering from Invalidation

This chapter will highlight some ways to get yourself motivated to validate your partner even when it seems very difficult indeed. It's especially important to be able to recover after your partner actually has been critical of you or responded to you in an invalidating way. Perhaps surprisingly, part of your motivation to validate what your partner is experiencing, wanting, or doing will come from validating your own experiences and desires. This chapter will also discuss how to get yourself to repair some of the damage after you have invalidated your partner. Ultimately, similar skills are required to proceed, whether you were the one being invalidated or the one who invalidated the other.

How to Validate Yourself

Self-validation is a very useful skill and strategy across a variety of sit-Uations (Fruzzetti1997, 2002; Fruzzetti and Iverson 2006; Linehan 1993a). Not surprisingly, you can use the ways that you validate others to validate yourself. To some extent, this is just an extension of mindfulness and awareness of yourself from chapter 2. You can simply pay attention to your experiences and behaviors, your emotions, sensations, wants, thoughts, and actions. You can then consider how to accept these things and use this self-acceptance and self-validation to achieve balance, which will in turn allow you to be more accurate in your expression and disclosure and therefore more validating toward your partner.

Be Aware of, Accept, and Describe Your Own Experience

At a very fundamental level, validating yourself is much the same as validating someone else. You must find a target to validate (something valid such as your emotions, desires, sensations) and respond to your own experience in a way that accepts and legitimizes it. With self-validation, it is just as important to stay away from judgments. Self-validating does not mean saying you are right instead of wrong or that anything you do is okay. Self-validation involves description: what are the facts? And self-validation, by letting judgments go, allows you to simply be in your own skin in the world. You exist. You are here. You know what you feel, want, or think (or that you aren't sure; "confusion" would then be the accurate word to describe your mental state). These are facts.

Whenever in doubt, turn to description. Describe what you feel, your sensations, what you want. Remember that these are *facts* : you feel whatever you feel, want whatever you want, think whatever you think, regardless of whether others might feel, want, or think the same way. Acting on those feelings, desires, or thoughts might be effective or problematic, however. The point is that by separating facts from judgments, you can then exercise greater self-control and act in ways that lead you to feel proud of, and not embarrassed about, yourself.

For example, you might want to spend more time or less time with your partner than she or he wants to spend with you. It is common in couples for there to be a difference in how much time they desire to be together, or how much intensity or closeness they share, and even small differences can be the trigger for a lot of pain and disagreement. Talking with friends can often make the situation worse, because in their quest to be supportive, they may fan the flame of judgments about your partner ("he's wrong" or "she's being unreasonable"), contributing to further polarization between you and your loved one.

The facts may be that you want what you want and that your partner wants something different. The difference could be large or small. There is no right or wrong to this. So self-validation would mean simply noticing what you feel and what you want, describing it to yourself (or to others), and accepting or acknowledging it as the fact that it is. Notice how accurate expression is, in reality, actually self-validating! This happy coincidence means that when you are working to be effective in communicating with your spouse or partner, you are also supporting and validating yourself.

PRACTICE

1. Practice noticing and describing your experience. What are your sensations? What are you feeling? What do you prefer to happen? These are facts, so state them as facts. No judgments!

2. Identify certain feelings or desires that you have related to conflict with your spouse or partner. Separate the facts (descriptions of your feelings and desires) from your interpretations or judgments. Practice just acknowledging that you feel what you feel and want what you want. If it is helpful, you can return to some of the skills in earlier chapters (see the discussion in chapters

2 and 3 on tolerating disappointment or allowing your emotion) and practice them some more.

Show Compassion Toward Yourself

If what you notice is that you are suffering, it may be self-validating first to describe your experience to yourself and then show tolerance and acceptance. We often judge ourselves, blame ourselves, and criticize ourselves. This can be a constant chatter of invalidation in our heads that creates a lot of negative emotional reactions and a lot of unnecessary suffering. Remember that when you are judgmental of yourself, you will feel embarrassed, guilty, or ashamed. Perhaps you have done something that did not work out well. Maybe you even did it out of mean-spiritedness. You can describe this with compassion toward yourself, especially if you are willing to work to repair the damage or work toward more self-control in the future.

Paradoxically, the more we judge ourselves for our behaviors, the more likely we are to behave in ways that are against our goals and values. The reason is that our self-invalidation creates heightened negative emotion (typically shame), which then interferes with our thinking and problem solving and makes us more reactive to negative (or even ambiguous) cues from our partner. So, if you beat yourself up ("I'm such an awful spouse. I should never have said that to her!"), you then feel awful (humiliated). And when your partner says something to you, such as "you were really mean and unreasonable," you already have all this negative emotion and maybe just can't stand more shame. So you quickly lash out at the "stimulus" for this increased pain: the very person you hurt in the first place. This, of course, makes you feel worse (more ashamed) later on, which again increases your angry response in the next argument, and so on, ad nauseam.

Strangely, self-understanding and compassion are the keys to breaking this cycle. Showing more compassion toward yourself will increase your ability to act with more compassion toward your mate. Understanding what you feel, want, and so forth, how you got there, and that you are not wrong to have these feelings or desires soothes your emotional arousal. You are not crazy. When your emotional arousal comes down, you can then work on acting in ways that are more effective and consistent with your goals and values, which will further reduce your humiliation (or other negative emotion).

You can also notice the ways in which your experiences and actions are valid. As discussed in chapters 7 and 8, there are many ways that what we feel or want or do can be valid. Our reactions may be normative, they may be learned through prior experiences, or we may not know how or why we feel or act the way that we do, but we can assume it would make sense if we had enough time and resources to figure it out. In which ways are your feelings valid? Just because others may feel differently does not mean you should. The fact is you don't. Or maybe anybody would feel the way you do or want what you want. Use description and compassion to sort out what you feel and what you want, and accept these for what they are: *your* valid feelings and *your* valid desires.

PRACTICE

1. Notice what kinds of things you tend to be self-critical about. Are these criticisms helpful? If they are nonjudgmental and help you organize your behaviors and act in ways that you feel good about, great. If the criticisms are not helpful, let go of the judgments and be descriptive.
2. Practice finding compassion for your feelings, even if they are feelings that make you uncomfortable. Accept your wants and emotions as they are in this moment.
3. Notice the ways in which your uncomfortable feelings or problematic behaviors are valid. The idea is not to use self-validation as an excuse not to change, but to be able to be clear about why your action made sense *and* why it is nevertheless a problem. Both parts are true.

4. Use your commitment to yourself and to your partner as motivation to practice whatever skills you need to handle your interactions more effectively.

Getting Yourself to Validate When You Don't Feel Like It

Now it should be clear that self-validation actually increases your ability to validate others. And validating others increases your ability to validate yourself. You can use this observation to motivate yourself to validate your partner, even when it is difficult, even when you have an urge to attack and invalidate. But first, consider what it means to be invalidating, because being invalidated by your partner (or yourself) is one of the most important barriers to validating him or her.

What Is Invalidation?

Responding in an invalidating way means that we communicate that what the other person is feeling, thinking, wanting, or doing is wrong or faulty or illegitimate or is just not worthy of our respect or attention. We convey this by not paying attention, minimizing feelings, criticizing in a judgmental way, telling another how he or she "should" feel or what he or she "should" want, showing disrespect toward the person in general (using a patronizing tone or response, acting superior, thinking or showing that you are "better" than another), being judgmental, showing mean-spiritedness or contempt for the person, or treating him or her as an incompetent human being.

There are hundreds or more ways to invalidate the very valid experiences people have. When we invalidate, we trigger defensiveness, disappointment, anger, self-doubt, shame, self-invalidation, and other negative experiences in the recipient. When we invalidate a loved one, we corrode our relationship and help the other person be miserable, which of course swings right back at us, because we also increase the chances that the other person will invalidate us in due course. So, invalidating someone you love is indirectly a great way to make yourself miserable.

Why Do We Invalidate the People We Love?

What we want from others is openness, understanding, and acceptance. When our expectations are far away from reality, it is especially hurtful. Nowhere is this more true than with a spouse or partner. This is supposed to be the person who will treat us the best in the world (that is, we want our partner to be this way). But, once our partner shows his or her imperfections, we feel mightily disappointed. The bigger the gap between what we want and what we get in that moment, the more emotion there is, and the more it hurts. Our culture does not support descriptive language about our disappointment in these situations, even though it would be very helpful. Instead, our culture models criticism and anger. And anger leads to judgments, and judgments ... well, judgments are invalidating. Then the cycle begins: one person is critical, judgmental, angry, and invalidating, missing completely the disappointment that really is her or his primary emotion so often. Notice that the first step can actually involve self-invalidation (not recognizing your own true emotion).

This inaccurate expression is received as an attack (which it is, in a way, of course), which triggers similar emotions and reactions in your partner. Thus, invalidation begets invalidation.

So, there really are only two things to do: minimize the first steps of self-invalidation, anger, judgments, and so on, or stop the cycle and respond to invalidation with compassion, acceptance, and validation instead of reciprocating invalidation.

Breaking the Invalidation Cycle

We all know, more or less, when we are invalidated. Our arousal goes up and we feel that uneasiness, that mixture of hurt, fear, and dislike associated with not knowing whether to run and hide or to attack. The urge to run probably comes from the hurt and the fear of further infliction of hurt. The urge to attack probably comes either from anger, which can result simply from a lot of pain, or from intense dislike mixed with judgments, or from fear, because anger can be a conditioned response to fear (we learn to attack instead of running to "safety"). In close relationships, this response may be heightened because we are caught off guard. Your partner is, after all, the one you love and who loves you, creating even in distressed relationships a kind of hope for good outcomes that is demolished during invalidation. The fall from grace can be particularly jarring. When the urge to run is bigger than the urge to attack, you may withdraw, and this may help reduce your reactivity. Still, you need to reengage your partner sometime, and the question is, will you do so constructively or on the attack? If the initial urge to attack is bigger than the urge to run, you need an immediate alternative strategy if you are going to break the cycle and restore peace to your relationship.

Thus, the signs that you are in the invalidation cycle are that your arousal is going up fast and that you have an urge to attack. There are several strategies that you can use, either very quickly or over time, to break out of the cycle: self-validation; self-soothing; mindfulness (nonjudgmental awareness of your partner); remembering your genuine goals and values; empathy; accepting reality as it is (that is, the situation is not how you want it to be); and generating hopefulness.

Validate Yourself First

Okay, so you are in the middle of an argument, and you desperately want your partner to understand you, agree with you, support you, love you, and validate you. But he or she is just as upset (hurt, fearful, disappointed, angry) as you are, and he or she is not showing any signs of validating you. So, if you don't validate yourself, who will? Validate your feelings by identifying your primary emotions. Look for disappointment and fear; consider hurt, frustration, loneliness, and shame. Remind yourself that it does make sense to feel those feelings when you are in conflict with your spouse or partner, when she or he is failing to understand or support you or, worse, when she or he is invalidating your emotions or your wants or actions.

Notice your urges to attack. Ride the urge out, like a wave: it may come back, but you don't have to dive into it. Allow it: don't buy into it, but don't pretend it isn't there or try to suppress it. Remember, the urge comes out of your high emotional arousal, so if you try to push it down, it will just push back, maybe even bigger. So just allow it to run its natural course. Then, validate how hard it is *not* to react in a big, negative, destructive way when you feel attacked by your partner. As you withhold your attack, notice your composure, validate your hard work, feel good about your effort.

Hopefully, after doing some of these things, you will notice that your emotions are receding a little bit and, with them, your urge to attack. At this point, perhaps you can notice what you really want in the big picture: to get along a lot better with this person with whom you are fighting. Remind yourself that this is the person you love, and that, indeed, she or he loves you. Hopefully, you will know this, even though she or he is not making it abundantly clear at that moment. Remember, neither are you—at least not yet! This is a way to validate that this hard work and pain is in the service of something important to you.

Soothe Yourself

You also can soothe yourself by showing self-respect and treating yourself like an acceptable human being. If you feel sad, imagine what you might do if a friend were feeling sad. Do the same for your hurt, fear, and so on. Does reassuring yourself help? Try it. Try something physical, like stretching out tense muscles or finding a more comfortable position to sit (standing is not optimal for relaxing). Take your shoes off, put on a comfortable sweater or cover yourself with a blanket, or take off a layer of clothing if you are too warm. Rub your eyes or temples or your feet gently. Get a cold drink (nonalcoholic) or a hot one. Imagine a happier time to come, after you can get unstuck from this invalidation cycle. Find something you can do that is soothing, that directly brings your arousal down.

Remember Your Genuine (Long-Term) Goals

Why do we get into close relationships? We certainly do not have intimate relationships to win arguments or to grind our partners into dust. Yet, sometimes we take that posture. It is important to regularly remind yourself of what you want: a loving relationship, a partner who loves and supports you and whom you love and support. Despite the many flaws in any relationship, this is the person you love. If you have read this far in the book, it is clear that you really do want your relationship to be better.

If you remember that this is the person you love and that you want desperately for your relationship to be better, ask yourself how attacking your partner is going to get you this. You know the answer: clearly, it will not. Only loving-kindness is likely to result in reciprocated loving-kindness. If you want to be treated in a loving way, rule out a counterattack. Stop, and consider more effective strategies, like finding a way to validate your partner and reverse the cycle.

Use Relational Mindfulness to Develop Empathy and Validation Potential

Notice how awful you feel. Notice how difficult it is to not attack, to find that loving person inside you who has been hiding. Now, notice that your partner is probably feeling *exactly* the same way. In many situations, you have both done hurtful things, even if one of you does not realize it or understand it. Perhaps your hurtful behavior was unintentional but resulted in your partner suffering anyway (like patting someone on the back who has a sunburn).

Ask yourself, "What is she/he experiencing right now? How badly is this person, my love, suffering?" This is simply being mindful of your partner, noticing what she or he is doing or feeling. Remember that his or her anger and attack urges come from the same place as yours: hurt, fear, disappointment, and suffering. Remember that, intentionally or not, you have contributed to your partner's suffering, and that you can, right now, help alleviate it by breaking the cycle. Instead of attacking and invalidating, you can become interested, nonthreatening, open to hearing his or her experiences, validating, and loving. Remember that you have the skills and ability to reduce your partner's suffering.

Accept Things as They Really Are (Not Necessarily How You Want Them to Be)

Finally, when we are really incensed, enraged, judgmental, angry, and attacking, we actually are acting in a world of our imagination, not the real world. That is, we are acting as though the world should be different from the way it really is. One nonrelationship example of this is when you are thirsty and put money in a soda machine, but the machine doesn't give you a drink and will not give you your money back. Perhaps you put in more money. It takes your money again and still fails to give you what you want (now, two drinks). The *reality* is that the machine is broken. It makes sense that you don't like it and that you wish it would work. But if you become enraged, kick the machine or pound on it, you are not accepting the reality. The more you try to defy reality, the more thirsty you will become, and the more likely you are to cause collateral damage (breaking a toe or hand, embarrassing yourself if someone sees you acting this way, or having trouble getting back to work or whatever you were doing because you are so upset and preoccupied—and still thirsty).

Relationships are the same, in principle. We have certain expectations of our partners. When we are disappointed, we can accept the reality of the situation (his or her imperfections, our own disappointments), or we can become enraged and attack. Unlike the soda machine, however, humans have memory and feelings and learn to attack back or even to attack preemptively. So, there is even more collateral damage in relationships when we go on the attack, when we fail to accept reality as it is.

The solution is to accept the reality of the situation, at least in this moment. At *this moment,* your partner is not doing what you want. Then you can validate both your wants and your disappointment that you are not getting what you want. If you keep trying to use extreme force to get a gentle response, you will continue to live in a dreamworld, one that is full of dissatisfaction and lacking in fulfillment. Accepting the reality of this moment, that things are not as you would like, is the most fruitful path toward improving the situation and getting more of what you want later on.

Finding Hope: The Validation Rule of Three

Clearly, being invalidated is painful, and breaking the invalidation cycle is difficult. However, there is hope. Research has shown that when couples are fairly happy, they are able to retaliate less often when criticized or invalidated. Validation holds a lot of promise as a way out.

Not only does validation work, but it works rather quickly. You can think of it as the validation rule of three. That is, if you can find the willingness, the courage, to validate three consecutive times in the face of invalidation, the other person almost always will stop the attack and his or her own negative reaction (invalidating responses) to you will begin to subside. Even if you know this, however, continuing to validate in response to a withering attack is not easy.

Veronica and Paul fought like cats and dogs. Despite clearly loving each other, they were highly sensitized to each other's judgments, criticisms, inattention, and other forms of invalidation. Having learned how to self-manage their emotions and how to validate each other, they practiced. When things were not too hot, they could slow down, express themselves clearly and accurately, and each was able to validate the other. This led to times of closeness that they fully enjoyed, much like earlier days in their relationship. However, if one of them became nasty or overtly critical in a big way, the other threw his or her skills down the toilet and jumped right in and matched the first one in negativity and invalidation. They would limp away from these arguments hurt, dazed, confused, and humiliated, both having behaved badly.

After discussing the validation rule of three, Paul decided to try it. He practiced it first in his head and rehearsed all of the things that motivated him to endure Veronica's attack and to respond in a more loving and validating way. It didn't take long for him to have his opportunity to try it out. They got into one of their usual rows, with Veronica criticizing Paul for being aloof and uncaring and Paul criticizing Veronica for being too sensitive and too critical. After a few turns in which each upped the ante, Paul remembered his commitment to do this differently. He took a deep breath, sat down, and tried to soothe himself. He self-validated: "Boy, this is harder than I thought. I'm really hurt and angry. But, now that I think of it, I'm also embarrassed that I was not very attentive to Veronica even after she told me she'd had a hard day and wanted my attention and support." He also remembered how lovely things had been the past couple of days, how much he really wanted their life to be more like that, less like this present argument. And he noticed how hurt Veronica was, how despairing she seemed, and realized how much pain she must be in to be so defensive, so attacking, so unlike her core nature, which Paul knew to be kind and loving.

He decided to try validating: "Veronica, I can see that you are really miserable doing this, and so am I" (this acknowledged her feelings and vulnerability, and reciprocated her vulnerability). She responded angrily, "Well, I'm glad you're as miserable as I am." But she noticed that something was different: maybe he wasn't attacking back? Paul continued, "I know you were really disappointed that I wasn't paying much attention, especially since you told me you had a crappy day at work." Veronica sensed the shift in Paul, but her emotions were still running a little high. She replied, somewhat bitterly, "Why didn't you say this twenty minutes ago? You're a little late, aren't you?" Then Paul said to himself, "Okay, one more try. I think I can do it." He said to Veronica, "I wish I had. I know you don't want to fight any more than I do. But I'm listening now, and I really want to hear what happened today." Veronica's anger and defensive diminished and, overwhelmed with sadness, she started to cry. She asked Paul to hold her. He did, and after a few minutes, her emotions came down, and she told Paul about her day. He listened, validated her, and she validated back how loved she felt that he had done what he did, how hard it must have been, but how important it was to her.

PRACTICE

1. Practice each of the six strategies described above. For each one, think of a recent situation in which you were at least a little bit invalidating. Try to find a way to use each strategy to help you break the invalidation cycle in a situation like this recent one.
2. Make a plan. Just as Paul did, identify what is important to you,

identify effective ways to self-validate and self-soothe, practice being mindful of your partner even when your partner is at his or her worst. Practice developing empathy for your partner in a situation in which she or he is verbally attacking and invalidating you. Work on accepting the reality of the situation: your partner sometimes does exactly the opposite of what you would like, but attacking or invalidating her or him will only make it worse. Practice being able to come back at least three times with a validating response even if your partner stays in the attack mode.
3. Implement your plan! Give it a try. Evaluate how it goes. If it turns things around, great. If not, what could you do better next time? Do you need more self-soothing? More self-validation? More rehearsal in your mind? Keep trying it. And don't get stuck on whether you should have to do all this. Remember to accept reality.

Repairing After Invalidation

Sometimes we do invalidate our spouse or partner. When we do, some kind of repair is required. Of course, we often feel that she or he invalidated first, which may be true. And, she or he often feels that we escalated and invalidated first, which may be true. There really isn't much utility in arguing about this. The reality is, if you were invalidating, you did some damage, and a repair is required.

Find the Motivation to Repair

To generate motivation, you need the very same skills that you would use to break the invalidation cycle: self-validation; self-soothing; mindfulness (nonjudgmental awareness of your partner); remembering your genuine goals and values; empathy; accepting reality as it is (that is, the situation is not how you want it to be); and generating hopefulness. So, the first steps are to reduce your arousal, find balance, and stay aware of your goals, while not succumbing to hopelessness. These prepare you to validate. But there may be three additional reasons to repair, whether immediately or some time later: it's the right thing to do, it will help jump-start your next interaction in a different, more constructive direction, and it will build your self-respect.

How and When to Repair

The earlier sections of this chapter focused on breaking out of the invalidation cycle while it is in full gear. That is critically important to do. And, to a great extent, when you validate in those situations, you are providing a repair for whatever invalidating responses you have recently thrown toward your partner. But the cycle can also be broken in other ways which typically begin by trying to bring your emotions back down to a moderate level and then by starting to repair prior damage.

Repair can be accomplished after an argument (or before the next one). Repair may be easier after an argument than during one because you have time to self-regulate your emotional arousal, to go through the steps above carefully, and to rehearse what you are going to say and how you will say it. Pick the most effective time and situation, just like you would for any effective expression (see chapter 6).

The repair itself can take many forms, but it will be most effective when it includes the following components: genuineness (find the part of you that *wants* to repair, that is, not doing it only because you are supposed to); mindful awareness of the impact of your invalidating behavior on your partner (notice how it must have felt, what the repercussions likely are, what suffering was involved); willingness to allow your partner to feel bad (don't expect your repair to undo the damage but, rather, to facilitate moving on); accurate expression and description of what you did and what you understand the impact to have been for your partner.

Also, to really repair the situation you need to commit to do whatever is necessary to have better self-control next time (that is, make a plan for improving your skills and self-control, and practice it). This will substantially reduce the chances of you invalidating your partner in the same way again. And, finally, you need to be ready and willing to validate your partner regardless of how he or she responds to your repair. That is, even if he or she is angry, blaming, or unresponsive, it is important to remember your goals and that he or she is still hurt from whatever you did that was critical or invalidating.

For example, Cameron and Charlie struggled with how much closeness they wanted in their relationship. One day, they had another big argument, and each was quite nasty to the other. Despite practicing the skills above and intending to stop invalidating, as well as hoping to break the cycle by validating, Charlie found herself escalating more, really saying awful things to Cameron. She was out of control and could not stop herself. Of course, afterwards, she felt terrible: sad, fearful, embarrassed, and ashamed. She decided to make a repair because it was the right thing to do (Cameron did not deserve to be treated that way), to try to improve the relationship (this might help both of them calm down and be more skillful next time), and to enhance her own self-respect (she had transgressed her own values, been mean and nasty).

Charlie waited until Cameron seemed settled and somewhat relaxed after dinner. She said, "Sweetie, I want to talk about our fight on Monday night. I just feel awful about it. I don't want to complain about you or try to talk about the issue. I just want to tell you how bad I feel about the things I said. Is this okay with you right now?" Cameron agreed, so Charlie continued, "I imagine that when I say really nasty things to you that it hurts you a lot. It would hurt me. It would hurt anyone. I imagine that you also feel kind of scared of talking more, maybe wanting to avoid me for a while. That's understandable, even though I really want to be closer to you, not farther away." At this point Cameron was softening up a bit, felt better, but did indeed feel inhibited and did not say anything. Charlie went on to say, "So,

I just don't want to treat you this way. What I'm going to do is take a little time out the next time we are having that kind of fight. Maybe I'll just take a couple of minutes in the bathroom and practice noticing you, noticing how much I love you. I think that will help keep me from getting so scared and keep me from lashing out at you. After a couple of minutes, we can talk more, if you want. What do you think? What else can I do to repair this?" Thus, Charlie started the process of repair and took it quite a few steps. Cameron proceeded to talk about the episode, and Charlie was open, warm, and validating. Cameron also noticed that Charlie followed through and did take occasional breaks during arguments, and he really respected and appreciated her for that. It helped Cameron's motivation to be more validating, in turn.

PRACTICE

1. Think about a moderately or significantly invalidating thing you have done recently. Go through the steps noted in this chapter to build motivation

to validate and repair and to reduce your negative emotion. Plan what your repair will look like. Rehearse the repair in your mind, anticipating how your partner might respond (including a negative response) and how you will continue with the repair.

2. Pick a good time and situation and implement your plan. Evaluate it and make adjustments as needed for the future. Follow through with whatever you need to do to increase your self-control and your skillfulness. Stay focused on your actions, what you need to do to make things go better in the future. And take a moment to notice your skillfulness and your commitment and to be content with your efforts and their results.

Chapter 10

Managing Problems and Negotiating Solutions

This chapter switches gears. Now that you are able to communicate fairly well, it may be useful to try to solve some of the problems that come up in your relationship. Most couples have a fairly good idea of how to do this, especially when they are getting along well. However, it may be useful to have a road map for managing problems and negotiating solutions to keep you on track. After discussing the concept of problem management (as opposed to problem solving), this chapter will lay out a set of steps that you can take to get clarity on your goals, solve whatever parts of the situation or problem you can, and manage whatever can't be solved so that it does no further damage to your relationship.

Problem Management Vs. Problem Solving

When you solve a problem, presumably the situation is changed fundamentally, such that the problem no longer exists (or at least it recedes for a long time). If the problem is that the roof leaks, you get it fixed, or you fix it yourself. You know the problem is solved, at least for a long while, and you don't have to pay attention to it anymore. If the first repair doesn't work, you may implement a more expensive or more comprehensive solution (maybe a new roof). After one or two tries, there is no longer a leak.

Most relationship problems are far more complicated than getting a leaky roof fixed, however. In those situations that can easily be solved ("Okay, I'll pick the kids up after school"), one or both partners do what is needed, and you move on. But most problems have a chronicity to them: you think you have solved the problem, but there it is again the next week. Relationship problems often take many, many attempts before they are solved (or resolved). Or, they can't be solved in any permanent or semipermanent sense but must regularly be addressed. A better approach might be to manage these problems, in the same way that you manage your finances: things are always changing; sometimes they are predictable, sometimes not. You know that even if you have enough money now, you may not next month or next year, depending on what happens (bills, income, job changes, unexpected expenses).

In addition, sometimes partners disagree about what the problem actually is. For example, one person might say the problem is "deciding who does the dishes" while the other says it is "fairness" in household chores. Clearly, these issues are related, but each might require a different solution. Sometimes you need to agree about the problem definition in order to solve it, but at other times it's sufficient to find a solution that simply satisfies both definitions.

At other times, it turns out that the problem really was one partner's emotion about the problem or situation, such as feeling misunderstood or that his or her desires aren't valued by the other. In these situations, the solution is accurate expression and validation, not necessarily making changes. For example, you might say the problem is that the distribution of chores around the house is unfair. But, after talking about it for a while, it may turn out that you really just felt unappreciated. Knowing that your partner is aware of all that you do and is really appreciative of it may render the problem moot.

For all of these reasons, it may be more useful to talk about negotiating solutions to problems when solutions are possible and desirable and about accepting problems (and validating each other's feelings about them) when solutions are not forthcoming. In other words, it might be more accurate to call this set of tasks *managing* problems.

Problem Definition

Most relationship problems involve one partner's desire for the other one to change. This, of course, is a solution, not a definition of the problem. For example, Kevin hates doing the laundry, so he thinks the problem is that he has to do the laundry sometimes. Alicia thinks the problem is that she does most of the household chores. Consequently, they fight about who does what quite often. What is the problem here? Or are there two separate (but related) problems?

It is impossible to know the answers to these questions until Alicia and Kevin sit down to discuss their feelings and their desires and are prepared to listen and validate each other's feelings and desires. Okay, so Kevin doesn't like doing the laundry. Alicia might be confused: "Why not?" She could be judgmental: "What's the big deal?" Or she could be validating: "You do seem really to dislike doing it. Why? What about it is so difficult or unpleasant?" It turns out that Kevin is a mechanic, so he has his hands in engines all day. They get very dirty and he uses very strong soap to get them clean, and his hands are always chapped and sore. Doing the laundry actually makes his fingers more chapped, and they sometimes split open and bleed, which interferes with his work, besides being painful. Alicia never knew this. She is very accepting and validating: "I wish I had known this. You poor thing!"

Alicia might respond in one of several ways. In scenario one, Alicia accepts the situation, agrees to do the laundry, and does not resent it because she understands that it really is hard on Kevin. Notice that this actually would give Alicia more chores, and her complaint was that she already did too many! But, this might be okay with her because she understands Kevin's objections to the laundry now, and Kevin is happy because he no longer has to do laundry.

Alternatively, in scenario two, Alicia might want Kevin to do something else, a kind of trade: "I'll do the laundry—how about you do the vacuuming and clean the bathroom?" From here, they move to negotiation. Alicia's willingness to take on the laundry chores helps Kevin be willing to take on other chores in exchange. Both leave the situation feeling okay.

In scenario three, Alicia is very sympathetic to Kevin's skin problem. She suggests that he see a dermatologist, get some medicine to help his chapped fingers, and use more hand lotion. If she starts out the conversation with soothing and validating, then Kevin might be open to continuing to do the laundry, *assuming* that his hands improve. She could say, "Oh, honey, that's terrible! We need to get you some medicine. I'll call my sister—she has been really happy with her dermatologist, and maybe you can get an appointment there." However, if Alicia jumps right into problem-solving mode and stays focused on the laundry as her first priority, it probably won't go so well. Imagine Kevin's response if she said, "Well, if you take better care of your hands, maybe see a dermatologist and use more hand cream, doing the laundry shouldn't be such a problem for you." Kevin would likely not feel soothed or cared about, and his motivation to see the dermatologist would probably be no higher than his motivation to do the laundry. Kevin and Alicia will likely be arguing about this again next week.

These scenarios point to the importance of seeing problems not as static, easily solvable situations, but as ongoing and ever changing, and as requiring a lot of communication, clarification, self-awareness, awareness of your partner, and flexibility over time. It's great to try to define a problem. But don't be surprised if you do not agree about what the problem is. Try to talk about it openly, gently, and in a validating way. Using your communication skills will make it possible to proceed with increasing understanding, which will in turn make solutions more likely.

PRACTICE

1. Pick what you think is a small problem that has come up lately. Sit down with your partner and try to define what the problem is. Stay open-minded, and validate your partner a lot.
2. Notice how your idea about what the problem is changes over time,

both in response to your conversation about it and with heightened awareness of what is bothering you and what is bothering your partner.

Problem Analysis

Once you have some idea about the dimensions of the problem, at least from each person's perspective, it makes sense to try to understand the problem better. There are many ways to analyze a problem: talking about the issue in general, speculating on why it is a problem, analyzing a specific instance of the problem and so on. This method will emphasize being very descriptive and specific, noticing both the details about the context in which the problem occurs and the consequences of whatever behavior (or lack of behavior) somebody wants to be different. Sometimes this is referred to as "behavioral analysis" or a "chain analysis" because each step (or link) that leads to the problem can be identified (e.g., Barlow 1981; Haynes 1978; Linehan 1993a). Modifying any one link holds the potential for making an impact on the larger problem.

One way to do this is to pick a specific example of the problem's occurrence. Agree on a specific incident, a time and place, so you are both talking about the same thing. It may be helpful to write down the steps, perhaps on a sheet of lined paper. If you fold the paper into two columns, you can put your name at the top of one column and your partner's at the top of the other. This way you can see both how the problem unfolded for each of you individually and how you interacted along the way.

You start by identifying what emotions you brought to the situation, especially the ones that really had nothing to do with the problem at hand. Then, each partner notes his or her feelings, thoughts, reactions, and so on in their column, starting at the top and going in sequence, and synchronizing with each other. On the crease of the paper (middle), you write down what was actually said or specific actions taken (such as eye rolling, walking away, or gently picking up and caressing the other's hand). This makes public what was going on inside each partner (thoughts, feelings, desires) and therefore allows both partners to see how, and often why, each one reacts to the other.

For example, Janelle and Trey argued regularly about money: how much to save, how much to spend, what to buy, and so on. Every time they tried to talk about it, they reached an impasse, even when they were skillful and respectful and mostly validating. So they decided to try to analyze the problem.

They agreed to take a detailed look at their argument from the previous Saturday morning. Here is what their chain analysis looked like:

As they looked at the chain of events together, Janelle and Trey were shocked to see how much of the problem was not about the money but about how they talked and reacted to each other. They each were able to acknowledge how the other might be hurt or might reasonably react the way they did at each step of the argument. What emerged was the clear sense that both of them were worried about money and both wanted to get their bills under control. However, Janelle did not want Trey "dictating" the solution to her. Rather, she wanted to work out an agreement that would affect them both. They came up with a budget that allowed each of them the same amount of discretionary spending money per week. Trey thought the problem was solved because this stopped the negative flow of money; he felt that it was a fair solution and that Janelle was taking the problem seriously. Janelle thought it was a good solution because she did not have to "feel under a microscope" about money. She knew what she could spend or save and that she had complete control over that. She felt much more respected by Trey. (Figure 7a & 7b)

Janelle	Trey
Tired, stressed	Anxious, worried that Janelle's mad at him
J: "I'm going to the mall with my sister in a few minutes. I'll be back before dinner."	
	Remembers their credit card bill, gets worried about money
	T: "You know, we're almost broke. Maybe you shouldn't be going to the mall today."
Thinks, "He's got some nerve telling me not to spend money, after he just went out and bought himself a bunch of CDs last week." Feels hurt, angry.	
J: "Well, you thought we had enough money to buy CDs, so I guess I think we have enough money for me to go to the mall."	
	Feels guilty, then gets judgmental, thinking, "She's being a real jerk about this," then angry
	T: "You are so irresponsible about money! I work my butt off and you couldn't care less. We'll never get out of debt, and it's your fault. You leave it all up to me!"

Figer 7a

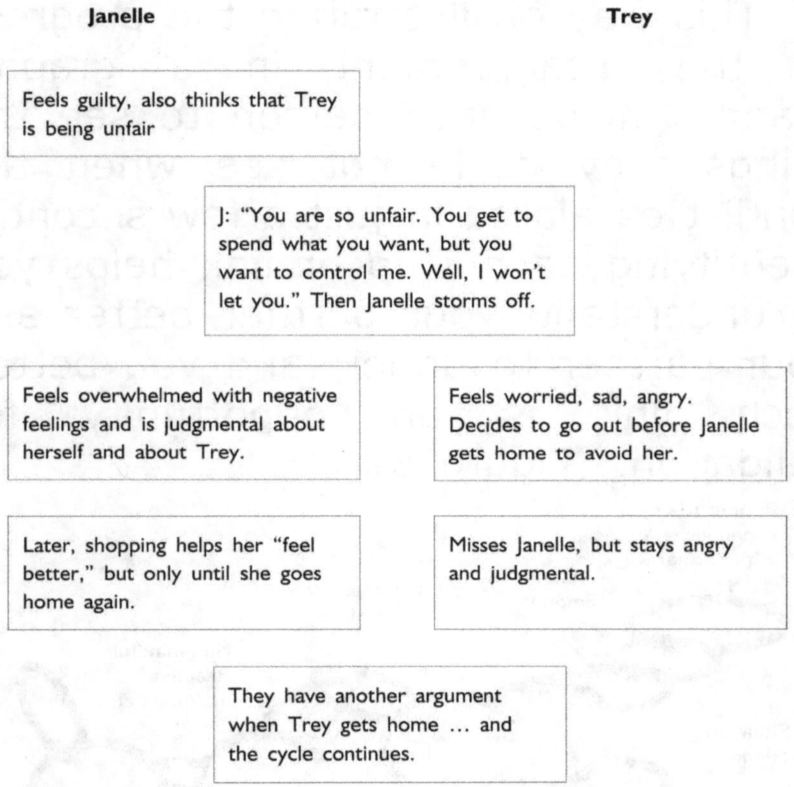

Janelle   **Trey**

> Feels guilty, also thinks that Trey is being unfair

> J: "You are so unfair. You get to spend what you want, but you want to control me. Well, I won't let you." Then Janelle storms off.

> Feels overwhelmed with negative feelings and is judgmental about herself and about Trey.

> Feels worried, sad, angry. Decides to go out before Janelle gets home to avoid her.

> Later, shopping helps her "feel better," but only until she goes home again.

> Misses Janelle, but stays angry and judgmental.

> They have another argument when Trey gets home ... and the cycle continues.

Figure 7b

Another way to do the step-by-step analysis is to draw out a chain of the steps, as shown in figure 7. Each person has his or her own thoughts and emotions occurring, which are private. These lead to statements and expressions that are public. In the figure, the private steps or links are open or clear, and the public ones are shaded.

This way of illustrating the progress of the disagreement in a graphic manner helps each person to see the things they could not see when the conflict escalated in just a few seconds. Identifying each step or link helps you to understand your partner better and your partner to understand you better. Each link is an opportunity for validation. (Figure 8)

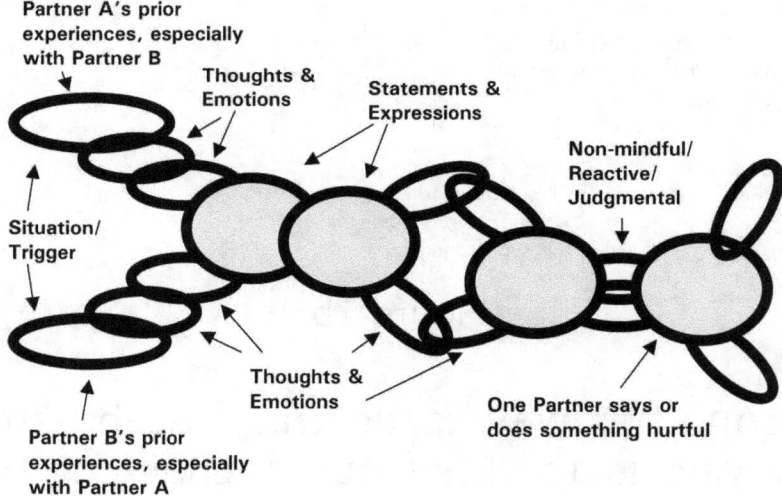

Figure 8

PRACTICE

1. Pick a small disagreement you have had recently, and do a problem or chain analysis of that disagreement. What happened? List or draw your

thoughts and emotions as well as what you said and did. Discuss the chain and use each "link" as an opportunity to expand your understanding of your partner. Validate your partner's emotions and desires and other reactions along the chain.
2. After you have successfully completed the first step (it may take several tries), move on to a bigger problem, and follow the same steps. Don't worry about solving the problem yet. Just use this exercise to enhance your understanding of the problem and the process of your disagreement. Validate!

Acceptance as an Alternative to Change

So far, this chapter has examined problems that at least had initial solutions. When solutions are possible, then negotiation and change are effective steps to take. However, sometimes a couple can "solve" a problem over and over, and yet it keeps coming back. In these situations, it may be prudent to consider just accepting that you have the problem; you may be able to fix it at some point but probably not right now.

Acceptance is hard. If neither partner were bothered, there would be no need to work on a solution. So, acceptance means that one or both of you will still be bothered. However, sometimes the solution can become part of the problem. Maybe the budget that Janelle and Trey agreed on was unrealistic or too hard to stay within, and they kept fighting about money, with Trey nagging Janelle and Janelle getting defensive in return. Sometimes problems develop a life of their own, and even the idea that you don't have to solve it right now can be freeing and lead to relief and allow you to connect and enjoy other parts of your life for a while. This issue will come up again in chapter 11, but for now it may be useful just to consider the possibility, when facing an intractable situation that is draining your energy and goodwill, that the problem is not such a big deal and that maybe you could just tolerate things the way they are for a while.

Change: Steps in Negotiating a Solution

As the example of Janelle and Trey demonstrates, two or more different problems often emerge: usually at least one is the conflict topic (being in debt or who gets to decide how much you spend), and the other usually is the conflict process (how the couple ends up arguing about money, how it becomes toxic). It is important to agree, and be clear, about which part of the conflict you will focus on resolving or managing. Trey and Janelle were able to address their conflict content (money) only after finding a much better, more constructive conflict process. This is quite typical.

Focus on One Conflict Topic at a Time

After doing a problem or chain analysis, the next step is to list your conflict topics. This might start out as only one topic, but could end up encompassing a lot of things, particularly after you do a chain analysis and gain some insight into the conflict process. Just keep a list, and make sure you are focusing on only one topic at a time. This is your target. Stay focused.

After starting to list your conflict topics, and before you try to resolve any of them, you must find a healthy, effective process. Use the chain analysis in two ways: identify your own reactions, judgments, and other unmindful behaviors, and use your skills to prepare yourself to act and react differently the next time; and go over the links or steps with each other, using all the validation skills outlined earlier in this book (from attentive listening to finding the "of course" in how he or she reacted that way). When you understand your partner better, it is easier to respond in a more loving, less reactive way. When you are able to talk about the actual topics without escalating into a lot of negative emotions and without either shutting down or invalidating the other, you are ready to try to find and negotiate solutions.

Brainstorm Possible Solutions

For your first problem topic, start to imagine what you could do to improve the situation or solve the problem (e.g., Jacobson and Margolin 1979). It may be helpful to start the discussion by offering a solution for which you would primarily be responsible. Although this may not always be possible, when you do this, you are communicating your commitment to solving the problem rather than your commitment to getting the other person to change. Effective solutions will likely involve changes for both partners.

It is common for one or both partners to have an idea about how to solve the problem. However, remember that your solution is just one possible solution: stay committed to solving the problem, not committed to a particular solution.

It may be helpful to keep a list of possible solutions as you come up with them, and you should also write down things you could do that might facilitate solutions. Brainstorm many possible solutions. Stay openminded, be creative, and don't be afraid to seek help from other sources (friends or relatives, books, the Internet). Just be sure that whenever you discuss the problem with someone else that you do not use the discussion as an opportunity to practice self-righteousness or to criticize your partner. And make sure that your partner is comfortable with you discussing this particular problem with other people. If not, keep it between the two of you. Finally, remember that this may take time. Only work on it as long as your attitude is constructive and your emotions are moderate. It is okay to take a break for a few minutes or even for a few days. The problem has been around a long time, so it may take a few tries to find a good solution.

Chloe and Ethan argued routinely about child rearing and parenting styles. Chloe thought that Ethan was too demanding and authoritarian with their two children, and Ethan thought that Chloe was too lackadaisical and permissive. But they both agreed that their differences were making things difficult for the kids, which helped motivate them to work on this problem together. They followed the plan outlined above and completed a chain analysis of a recent argument. They walked through it together, both identifying what they could do to make the process more constructive and validating each other. In this particular situation, their six-year-old son Caleb was whining about not wanting to do his chores (clearing his plate from the table and then putting his clean, folded clothes in his drawer in his room). As usual, Chloe wanted to reassure Caleb, gently nudge him to do his tasks, and reward him afterwards with a clear display of appreciation: "Great job, you did it. I'm proud of you." Also as usual, Ethan wanted Caleb to stop whining and just do his job. Caleb wanted both parents to ignore the whining and simply remind him to get his chores done. And, if Caleb didn't do his chores as directed within a certain amount of time (fifteen minutes), Ethan would prefer to take away a privilege, such as saying "no TV tonight." Ethan and Chloe decided to try to brainstorm some possible solutions to their conflict about how to parent Caleb. Here is a partial list of solutions they came up with:

1. Whoever assigned the chore would get to handle it the way she or he wants.
2. They would take turns handling the situation.
3. They would go to a child therapist or parenting class and agree to follow the expert's advice.
4. They would flip a coin and try it the winner's way for a month and then reevaluate; if Caleb was more responsive, they would keep that solution; if worse (or not better), they would try the other's.
5. They would get a point chart for Caleb, and every time he did his chores without whining or complaining, he'd get a point; these would be exchanged later for special playtime or fun activities.
6. Regardless of the rest of the solution, if Caleb continued to whine and not do his chores, he would not be able to watch TV or

do other privileged activities until his chores were completed.
7. They would hire a nanny to handle these situations.
8. Either parent could offer some "cheerleading" to Caleb to help him stay focused.
9. They would stop worrying about whose parenting was right and focus on the fact that Caleb was a generally happy and well-behaved little guy; maybe they only needed to stop fighting about the details.

As you can see, this is a wide-ranging list. The real list included quite a few additional suggestions. In reality, neither Chloe nor Ethan were advocating positions very different from leading parenting experts. The experts disagree, too! Of course, if one parent really was extreme to the point of harm (extremely permissive or extremely authoritarian; cf. Baumrind 1971), it might make sense to get a book or seek out an expert's advice. But, many of these kinds of arguments really are about style and about our own upbringing, our own fears and vulnerabilities. By generating a long list of possible ways to handle the problem, each was able to hear more about the other parent's concern and to validate.

For example, Chloe remembered being yelled at a lot by her father, and she remembered feeling very bad about herself as a result. So, when Ethan was firm with Caleb, even though objectively he was not being mean or doing anything close to being abusive, Chloe felt uncomfortable; she identified with Caleb and wanted Ethan to be gentler. She didn't want Caleb to respond to Ethan the fearful way she had to her father, and she didn't want to behave with Caleb the mean or critical way her father had behaved with her. Ethan, on the other hand, was thinking about his seventeen-year-old nephew with drug problems. Ethan had always cringed because his sister and brother-in-law never seemed to set any limits or enforce any rules with the young boy, even when he was rude or obnoxious or doing things that made other kids not want to play with him. He worried that Chloe might be "coddling" Caleb and that he would learn no self-control, no discipline, and no self-respect, and subsequently have a lot of difficulties in his life. Fortunately, this discussion between Chloe and Ethan was loaded with interest and validation. Afterwards, they felt a lot closer, a lot more like partners in parenting, even before coming to any solutions. They understood each other better, which resulted in increased trust and reduced worry.

Negotiate an Agreement

The next step is to negotiate. You can do this immediately after generating possible solutions, or you may want to take a break before moving on to this step. First, go over each possible solution on your own. Which solutions do you like, and why? What are the pros and cons (advantages and disadvantages) to each? Then, walk through each one out loud, with each other, sharing the pros and cons of each that you thought about. If there are solutions that you both agree have no redeeming value, cross them off the list. Among those that are left, can you piece together an agreement that includes useful parts from more than one solution?

As with the other steps, negotiation requires patience and perseverance. Make a proposal to your partner and evaluate it together. Don't be afraid to do some horse trading: "If you would be willing to do X, then I would be willing to go along with Y." There is no right solution. There are solutions that work, at least in some ways, and those that fail. Don't worry, if the solution you pick fails, you can come back to this step, analyze what went wrong, and hammer out a new agreement.

If you cannot agree, it may be useful to change your goal. Perhaps the problem you are trying to solve is too big, and you can carve out a piece of it to work on. Or, perhaps you need to resolve another problem before you can agree on a solution to this one. These are normal things to go through. What is most important is that you stay committed to being effective in your communication, with accurate, clear self-expression and bountiful validation, and committed to a solution that both of you find acceptable.

Commit to Your Agreement

At some point, you will find an agreement that is acceptable to both of you. It really helps to write it down, because with so many possible solutions flying around, you could think you are agreeing to one thing while your partner thinks he or she is agreeing to something else. So, write it down, clearly. Then, drop the discussion for at least twenty-four hours. Let the agreement settle. Then, return to the table and review your agreement. If it still seems acceptable to you both, you can move to implementation. However, do not be surprised if the agreement looks a little bit different after twenty-four hours. It might look better, or it might no longer seem acceptable. Do not despair; this is quite common! This means, of course, that you are back to negotiating (in good faith, of course; no invalidation, please).

It is important to specify exactly what you expect from each other. The point is not to evaluate each other but to be clear and be able to make a fully informed agreement. Now it is time to implement the agreement, so agree on a time frame: when does the agreement start?

Finally, set a time to take a look at whether the agreement is working out as planned. The idea is to set this far enough in the future so that you can relax and not feel a ton of pressure to succeed, but soon enough to be able to make adjustments to maximize the chances of it working. Right now is the time to decide the following: "How will we know whether the plan is working? What criteria will we use? What would tell us that it is a complete success? A partial success? A complete failure?" Agree on this now.

Evaluate Whether the Agreement Is Working and Fine-Tune as Needed

When the time to evaluate comes, it is important once again to bring your genuineness to the conversation. This is not a time for gloating over success or failure, nor is it a time for blame, "I told you so" statements, or to feel embarrassed that your ideas did not work out as you'd hoped. Rather, this is a time to experience the outcome together. It was your plan as a couple, so you sink or swim together.

The reality is that many plans fail the first time and, often, the second and third times. You are competent people. If the problem were easy to solve, you would have solved it a long time ago. Rather, the problem is sticky, complicated, and/or full of emotion triggers, so it is hard to solve, and that means it may take several tries.

The most effective thing to do is to evaluate how well the plan worked, based on the criteria you established when you made your agreement. If it worked, pat each other on the back; you did a great job and were lucky. If your agreement did not work out well, try to figure out what went wrong. Maybe do a problem or chain analysis of what did not work. Analyze the situation a bit more, go through the whole process again (don't worry, this time is usually faster), and negotiate a new agreement that benefits from what you learned in the recent failed agreement. Recommit, set a time (and criteria) for evaluating future success or failure, and repeat as needed.

Negotiating solutions can take a long time. But, as is evident from the steps in this chapter, there are many side benefits along the way: there are many opportunities to understand each other better, to express yourself clearly and accurately, to validate each other, and to act as a team solving a problem together, rather than as two people fighting each other as though the other person were the problem.

PRACTICE

1. Practice all the steps involved in negotiating solutions. Start with a small problem, one that at least seems as though you can solve it. Don't worry if it turns out to be bigger than you thought. Take each step in turn. And use mindfulness of yourself and your partner, emotion self-management, accurate expression, and validation all along the way.

2. Evaluate how you did as a couple solving the problem. Identify what each of you can do to make it go more smoothly the next time.
3. Pick another small problem and do the same. Continue with small problems until you are really able to work as a team.
4. Take on increasingly more complex or more emotion-laden problems, carefully following the steps and assiduously validating each other at each step.

Chapter 11

Transforming Conflict into Closeness

The end of this book is near. You have practiced the skills and procedures described so far. Maybe you have practiced a lot, maximizing your skills as a partner and a couple. Hopefully, you've experienced a big difference in the quality of your interactions and the quality of your life. However, it is likely that you still have problems. This is not your fault or your partner's fault. Life simply includes problems. The purpose of this last chapter is to help identify ways to let go of the suffering that accompanies whatever problems you still have. By using the skills already learned, but in a slightly more sophisticated way, you may be able to transform leftover conflicts into closeness and use mindfulness and acceptance skills to more fully engage your partner, your relationship, and your life, finding peace in each other instead of frustration, and closeness in every step you take together.

What Is Suffering? The Problem of Nonacceptance/Nonchange

Every day includes a host of things that go the way we like and a bunch of things that do not. Some of these are quite important to us, and we become very attached to achieving certain outcomes. Caring about outcomes gives us the motivation to work hard to get what we want. Unfortunately, we may not have the skills to learn to want what we actually get. This is a seemingly intractable problem in many close relationships.

Many partners have ideas about how their relationship should be. Some people want to be active, engage in adventures together, sharing every step with each other. Others want their relationship to be a haven to which they can escape at the end of the day from a sometimes cold and painful world. There are many, many notions about what form a good, healthy, close, and supportive relationship should take. So, we look for a mate who seems to share our vision, and we are excited when we find him or her.

However, first we forget that we have hundreds, perhaps thousands, of ideas about how we want the world, our relationship, our child rearing, as well as our cars, diet, budget, sex, laundry, and toothpaste caps, to be: no two people are the same. Secondly, we forget that nothing is constant except change: the world is constantly changing, as are we, so even enormous similarities with your mate at one point in time do not ensure that you will be so similar at a later time. In most situations, you might call this growth and change. But when it involves things you are attached to, it feels like loss, grief, sadness, and aloneness.

Thus, we have a fundamental choice. We can fight the changes around us (especially in our partner) or accept them. Change requires a lot of effort and often a lot of compromise, and therefore, it involves a certain amount of pain (adjustment pain, sadness over loss and change, and so on). That pain may be experienced first by your partner, who changes in response to your desire. You are relieved (perhaps you get what you want), but when you are mindful of him or her, you also experience some of his or her pain of loss (she or he had to change, give up a preferred way). Of course, change also can be quite invigorating and fulfilling. But with every new excitement, by definition, something previously cherished is lost, at least in a way. In addition, there is a certain amount of pain that results from acceptance: we recognize that something we were formerly attached to is now different, transformed, or lost, and we are sad. So, with acceptance or change, there is pain. This pain is part of living life well.

Suffering, on the other hand, results when we are stuck and cannot effectively change things to our liking, nor can we accept them as they are. This position of nonacceptance/nonchange is one of suffering not only because of the frustration of not getting what we want but also because of the discomfort associated with nonacceptance; we still are attached to the changes we desire. Moreover, this suffering can grow like a black hole to suck in everything around it, warping time, so that nothing in your relationship or your life seems okay and you stop living in the present. Nothing seems peaceful. There are big gaps in closeness with your spouse or partner. You suffer and your partner suffers with you, and your relationship suffers. This suffering is mostly unnecessary.

The previous chapter addressed many ways to achieve the changes you desire. If you can change or get your partner to change so that you both get more of what you want, that's worth the effort and the pain associated with change. But what if you keep trying and can't get the situation, yourself, or your partner to change? What then? If you stay attached to the idea of change, but cannot achieve change, you are stuck in nonacceptance/nonchange. You will be tempted, because you are still attached to the idea of change (it's the right thing, you can't imagine living any other way), to continue to think that the solution is bigger, better, more powerful change strategies. Well, good luck! The issue is *not* that you should not continue trying to get what you want. You have every right to do so. Rather, the issue is what the cost to your life, to your relationship, is going to be if you continue to try to get your partner to change. The following sections will consider the other alternative: acceptance of what actually is, even though you may not like it at first.

Finding Acceptance and Closeness

Sometimes you clearly want to focus on change. That's fine, of course. But, occasionally there is conflict; your partner does something that you want him or her to stop (or does not do something that you want), that is so consistently present and so resistant to change that you know in the back of your mind that continuing to try to get your partner to change has not worked and is not likely to work. But you really want your partner to change! And change is not happening, is not likely to happen. This nonacceptance/nonchange is driving you a little crazy.

What kinds of things fall into this category? In principle, anything your partner does that you don't like, as long as it is not contrary to your true values, is ripe for *either* effective change efforts or genuine acceptance. Maybe it's the way your partner parks the car in the garage, leaves the toilet seat up (or down), wants to be alone for a few minutes when she or he comes home (even though you are longing to talk about your day and want to be held), gets easily disappointed or hurt when you want some alone time, parents your children, is lackadaisical about something you care deeply about, or leaves his or her dirty socks on the stairs. It could be anything that you have tried and tried to get your partner to change. But your efforts have been in vain and change has not occurred. Pick one of these things and *consider* the following steps or exercises as an alternative to the usual nagging, complaining, anger, frustration, or bitterness you direct toward your partner about this particular behavior (Fruzzetti and Iverson 2004). You can opt out and return to a change focus at any time that you want to, without penalty.

Behavioral Tolerance

The very first step toward possible acceptance is to stop putting energy into changing your partner (at least this one behavior). Although this may sound simple, it's not. There are two main reasons that it is difficult to let go of your change focus or "change habit," even for a few days or a few weeks: first, tolerating a situation or behavior which you want to be different is painful; and second, letting go of your "change energy" means you initially will feel disappointed because you are facing the reality that you are not getting what you want. You are experiencing a loss.

The first step involves noticing all the ways that you try to get your partner to change this particular behavior. Do you nag, complain, or write scathing notes or e-mails about the "problem" behavior (or lack thereof)? Spend a few days and monitor all the verbal and nonverbal signals (including "looks that could kill") you send to your partner about this. Keep a written log, so you do not miss any of the many ways you put effort into getting him or her to change.

Now, stop them all, at least for now. Pick a time period, for example, three weeks, and commit to simply letting your change goals go for that time. No nagging, no complaining, no carefully timed wincing, eyes rolling, ugly quid pro quos, or other efforts to get him or her to do what you want on this one behavior. It's a cease-fire. You must do this unilaterally: do not even tell your partner. This is for you, not for him or her. Sure, she or he might feel relieved that you are off his or her back about this, but you are not doing it to be nice to your partner. If you choose to try this, you are doing it because *you* are stuck and willing to try a different strategy. The old strategies have not worked, so perhaps this path will lead someplace new and more peaceful.

However, in order to do this, to stop trying to get your partner to change, you must be able to deal with the emotions that will likely follow (intense disappointment) and the judgments and anger that likely will grow out of your frustration over not getting what you want.

Manage Disappointment

Disappointment is in the same emotional class as sadness and grief and so is quite similar. When you fail to get what you want, regardless of the reasons, disappointment is at least one of the emotions you are likely to feel. Disappointment can sting. It often brings with it fairly low energy and an urge to shut down or withdraw, to give up (at least temporarily). There are at least three important responses that help disappointment run its natural course so that you do not get stuck in sadness and depression:

1. Validate the disappointment: it makes sense when you don't get what you want; you can validate the feeling yourself, or let someone else do it.

2. Soothe the pain: treat yourself decently, do the kinds of things you might do for someone else temporarily feeling a lot of sadness, or get someone else to soothe you.
3. Get active: being active is a bona fide treatment for depression (Addis and Martell 2004), and likely an essential ingredient in preventing sadness from growing into depression. Getting active includes engaging in physical, social, intellectual/cognitive, and recreational pursuits, and pushing yourself to do a little more than perhaps you feel like. Activation not only distracts you away from negative emotional states, it also creates positive ones: when you engage the world, you do things that are enjoyable, the surest antidote to sadness and disappointment.

As you go over your checklist of how not to nag or complain or put energy into getting your partner to change, notice the disappointment, self-validate, self-soothe, and get active, especially with your partner.

Let Go of Frustration and Anger

You may also notice a cascade of quite judgmental thoughts about your partner as you go cold turkey and give up (at least temporarily) your change habit. You might think things such as, "Why should I have to feel this crappy? I wasn't asking for very much here. She or he should just change; it's not a big deal." Notice how these judgments and invalidating statements make some sense. In a way, they are quite seductive, especially when the alternative is tolerating your negative emotions. Similarly, when you make these kinds of judgmental statements about your partner, you will generate a lot of anger. And, when you're angry, your thoughts will tend to be judgmental. Try to observe this pattern: it is normal, makes sense, and is quite destructive. You may have the urge to go back to your old focus concerning change toward your partner when you feel this bad. However, you have made a commitment to quit nagging and tolerate what follows. The withdrawal symptoms you are experiencing will pass.

Annie and Seth used to fight a lot, but had worked hard and had vastly improved their relationship. However, there still were certain things that each of them did that drove the other crazy. Despite repeated pleas for change, several complicated attempts to use the problem management and negotiation skills found in chapter 10, and clear expressions of despair, each of them just couldn't seem to do what the other wanted in a few key areas. For example, Seth would often (a couple of times per week) play with their two-year-old daughter, Kara, and get her really excited just before bedtime. This made it hard for her to fall asleep and resulted in her bouncing out of bed several times before settling down and then being tired the next morning. Annie would become furious at Seth when she heard him and their daughter roughhousing throughout the house, but by then, it was too late. But she still scolded Seth and pushed him over and over to play quietly at bedtime and save the romping around for earlier in the day.

Annie, on the other hand, had a habit of misplacing things, such as losing keys (hers or Seth's), locking herself out of the house or car, or leaving her wallet or purse in restaurants. Often, she needed Seth to "rescue" her and the kids, which was disruptive for Seth (he might have to leave work to let Annie and the kids into the car at the grocery store, when she had locked her keys in the car, for example). He really resented these episodes and pressed Annie hard to manage her keys and wallet better.

It is obvious that neither Annie nor Seth is a bad person. Both are quite responsible adults, good parents, and mostly loving partners. Yet, each has some rather problematic behaviors in their repertoires. Their foibles might drive a lot of people crazy. What should they do? They have tried and tried to get the other person to change, over and over again, without success. Each of these situations is perfect to try stopping the old habit of nagging and complaining and resenting the other, and instead tolerating the other's behavior that has been driving him or her crazy.

Annie decided to stop nagging and criticizing Seth about his exuberant play at bedtime with their daughter. She went cold turkey, and kept a log on an index card of each situation in which she had an urge to yell at Seth. It turned out there were many. She practiced noticing disappointment and was surprised just how much sadness she felt when she let go of her judgments and anger. She had many judgmental thoughts run through her mind, however, such as "he's an adult, he should know better" and "he is so inconsiderate" and "he's just acting like a twoyear-old himself." But she persevered. She self-soothed: when she heard them start to roughhouse, she sat in her favorite chair, put on her favorite CD, and just relaxed and enjoyed a song or two. She selfvalidated in a variety of ways: she noticed her sadness and noticed that it made a lot of sense given that her ideas about how their parenting would go were not working out, and she validated how hard it was not to simply go with the urge to criticize Seth. And Annie stayed active, being sure to do things with friends and to go out alone with Seth on dates and enjoy those times together.

After a few weeks, she really had stopped nagging, complaining, and criticizing Seth for his active play at bedtime with their daughter. She was proud of the accomplishment, but every time he did it, she still felt a lot of negative emotion and noticed really wanting him to just stop it. She decided to move on to the next step.

While Annie was going through this process, Seth independently decided to consider accepting Annie's forgetfulness. He realized that when Annie lost her keys, wallet, receipts, or whatever, that his very negative and critical response did not actually help her become less forgetful. He went through a recent example of needing to leave work to come home to let Annie into the car so that she could take their son Jacob to a doctor's appointment. He noticed that his emotions included not only frustration about interrupting work but also worry about what others might think of him and disappointment that he would have to stay a little late at work. To stop trying to get Annie to change would mean he would face occasional, similar frustration.

Surprisingly, he also noticed that it was hard to see Annie and the kids in the middle of the day for a couple of minutes and then have to return to work. He missed them! He noticed that he had been quite sad about that but that he'd missed it at the time because he was overwhelmed with judgments ("she's so selfish and incompetent") and anger. He practiced self-validating these emotions and decided to stop complaining about Annie's forgetfulness and to stop criticizing her for it.

After you have stopped focusing on change for a while (several days, maybe several weeks), it will become easier. You will adjust. However, your partner's behavior may still bother you a little (or a lot). If the behavior that used to drive you crazy no longer bothers you, then you have changed what had become a bad habit for you. Congratulations! You are done and can move on (and maybe try to accept a different "problem" behavior). However, if your partner's behavior still bothers you, it is time to go on to the next step and explore the consequences of your change habit.

PRACTICE

1. Make a list of the things that you have tried, over and over, to get your partner to do differently, but without success.
2. Pick one that you are willing to tolerate for a couple of weeks.
3. Stop criticizing, complaining, nagging, demanding, or doing anything to try to get your partner to change.
4. Follow the steps suggested in this section to help you manage your disappointment and let go of your judgments and anger.
5. If you no longer are bothered by the behavior, give yourself some credit for effective habit reversal. And then go back to step two and pick another thing off your list, and continue on. If you are still

bothered, move on to the next section.

Become Aware of Unnecessary Suffering

To accept your partner's behavior fully, you will need a lot of motivation. Acceptance is not intuitive, and the default is change, change, change. In this step, you will pay close attention to the *cost* of your agenda of change, becoming more aware of how much suffering your nonacceptance/nonchange position causes.

You already have logged the situations in which you have had to work in order to tolerate your partner's behavior. Tolerating it has not been enough. It still eats away at you sometimes. What are the costs of leaning toward change, expecting change, wanting change?

In each situation in which you have to inhibit yourself from criticizing your partner or nagging or complaining, notice what happens. First, for however long you are "tolerating" your partner's behavior, you are unhappy, not engaged in the rest of your life: you are stuck in time, suffering. But it probably doesn't end there. Chances are good that for several more minutes (or hours), there are ripples of negativity that affect you, alter your experience, change how you interact with and feel about your partner (and others). The idea in this step is to formulate an accurate appraisal of all the costs of wanting your partner to change. How many minutes per day are you bothered? What are the consequences of your negativity? Economists call these costs *response costs*—the costs of responding in a particular way, in this case staying stuck on changing your partner. Also, what might you have done instead with that energy? These are *opportunity costs*—the things you weren't able to do because you were negative, sullen, angry, judgmental (lost opportunities for peace, relaxation, closeness, and enjoying each other).

Start a new log. Each time you feel sad, disappointed, frustrated, or angry, and you notice yourself being judgmental about this particular target, write it down. What happened next?

How long was it before you forgot about it? And, after that, how long before your emotions came back to equilibrium? What are the response costs? The opportunity costs?

The consequences of disappointment and anger might include the following: being more vulnerable to conflict about something else (you were "primed" for an argument); feeling more emotional distance from your partner; missing (not noticing, not responding, not enjoying) other things your partner might do; more misery for your partner, because he or she might still pick up inexplicable negative signals from you, even though you are not actively trying to get him or her to change; more negative feelings and misery for you; and inhibition that you or your partner feel toward each other. Add up the costs of these.

If the costs are low, you probably don't want to go on to the next step, for it is a particularly difficult step. It actually is more like a mountain. What's on the other side is wonderful, but if you are happy where you are, you probably do not want to put all that work into accepting your partner fully (it is hard to change ourselves). However, if the costs are very high, you might feel motivated to try the next series of steps, which involve actively putting your partner's behavior in a new context to create new meanings to attach to the behavior and new responses that are not full of suffering.

Annie kept the log for three weeks. She realized that her attachment to Seth doing what she wanted was pervasive. She thought about it many times on most days, and each time it left her with heightened emotional arousal. Consequently, she was a little less excited to see him when he came home, a little annoyed whenever he played with their daughter (regardless of when or how), and still just furious if their daughter had a hard time settling down and going to sleep. She realized she was particularly attached to the idea that her daughter should be in bed, asleep, by the same exact time each night, and that any minutes she was awake after that Annie implicitly experienced as an intrusion into her own downtime. Of course, all this makes sense, but they are still costs. Annie realized the costs were enormous and decided to try to let go of her change habit concerning Seth's bedtime playing style.

Seth looked back at the costs of his own intolerance. Looking back at the day when he'd left work to let Annie into her car, he realized he had been so judgmental and critical of Annie that she was distant and hurt when he came home later on. Jacob and Karen were a bit out of sorts as well. Seth recognized that he was getting less and less of what he wanted (peace with Annie and a more loving home). As he kept his list, Seth became more mindful of Annie and of his own disappointments. It turned out that his criticisms of her had a much bigger and more longtanding impact than he had ever imagined. He decided to try to accept Annie as she was, forgetfulness and all.

PRACTICE

1. Keep the log described above. Add up the costs of your focus on change.
2. Decide if it is worth trying something new (and difficult). If so, go on to the next section.

Let Go of Suffering: Find Peace and Engage Your Life ... Now!

For a long time you have been thinking (or assuming) that the cause of all your suffering is your partner's failure to change. An alternative view that is equally valid (neither more nor less) is that the cause of all your suffering is your attachment to an impossible agenda, your unwillingness to accept reality (that change is neither easy nor forthcoming). Maybe the behavior that drives you crazy has many possible meanings just ripe for you to pick, but you have only seen it in one very negative way.

Recontextualize Your Partner's Behavior

One way to start is to recontextualize your partner's behavior. You are used to thinking about it in a particular way, only noticing the negative qualities associated with this particular trait or behavior she or he has. Open your mind. See a bigger picture. What do you love about your partner? What do you like about him or her? In what ways is this behavior that has driven you crazy actually an integral part of your mate? Maybe it is connected to what you like and love about your partner. The idea here is to recondition the so-called problem behavior: using your mindful awareness, intentionally put the behavior in a different context so that different aspects of the experience—real aspects—become more salient, and the problematic aspects become less salient. Or, to put it differently, notice and pay more attention to the things you have been missing that are important, and try to pay less attention to the things that are problematic. Purposely and consistently use mindfulness to control what you pay attention to; choose to pay attention to those aspects of the situation that get you what you want (peace, closeness, joy, satisfaction).

    Annie finally noticed that Seth adored their daughter and that he loved playing with her, was very attentive to her, and was a great dad. Annie loved the fact that he loved being a dad. Maybe Annie had been attached to the idea that Seth should be a perfect dad, which, of course, he was not, nor could he or anyone be. She also noticed that he loved her, that she actually had a loving, devoted, monogamous spouse who liked being home with her and their children. How great is that? He was alive, he was home, he was not out drinking or carousing. These things she no longer wanted to take for granted. By purposefully noticing these very real and truly important aspects of the situation, after a while the "disrupted" bedtime no longer seemed disruptive at all. Instead, it was just a fun night with a happy and excited child who needed a little extra help settling down. Annie began to wonder how she had been so stuck on Seth's behavior, why it had bothered her so much.

Seth also took the final steps and practiced seeing the rest of the situation. Typically, Annie was very attentive to Jacob, to Kara, and to him. She would often dissolve into the moment and become unaware of other things around her: the flip side of her absentmindedness about some things was her intense devotion to her family, her warmth and affection. She also, despite occasional lapses with keys and so on, managed to keep most of the day-to-day activities of the family in good order. She paid the bills, was keenly in tune with Jacob's and Kara's needs, and was very attentive to Seth and delighted to see him (especially when he was not critical of her). Seth began to see that occasional lost keys were a small part of a larger picture of a loving wife and mother who adored her husband and their children.

Find Other Meanings in Your Partner's Behavior

Another strategy involves looking deeply at your partner and his or her life to find ways to understand his or her behavior. How does this behavior make sense given his or her life experiences? Given your relationship and your relationship problems? Given the things that are important to your partner? This is quite similar to the task of finding ways to validate discussed earlier in the book. How does this behavior make sense?

Annie knew that Seth grew up in a family in which there was a lot of emotional distance, not a lot of fun, and hardly ever much play with his parents. She also knew that Seth wanted desperately to provide a different experience for his children. This was one of the things she really loved about him, his commitment to their kids. Maybe the active play at bedtime just "happened" because Seth was more focused on enjoying their daughter than on ideas about how bedtime should go. Maybe he was so mindful of playing with their daughter, of just being with her, that other things were just not salient to him. Maybe playing, staying in the moment, not worrying much about arbitrary rules of parent-child interactions, was what Seth needed to do to be sure that he was different from his own parents. All of these new meanings seemed quite legitimate to Annie, and all of them helped her let go of her nonacceptance/nonchange position and embrace acceptance. In acceptance, there was peace and newfound closeness with Seth.

Similarly, Seth was able to let go of his criticisms of Annie's forgetfulness, finally leaving his prior position of nonacceptance/nonchange. Through acceptance of his wife, he could see that many other qualities were present in Annie. Paying attention to those other qualities brought them much closer together and brought increased peace and happiness to both of them.

By following similar steps, you may be able to take something that has been a source of enormous suffering for a long time and alleviate some of that suffering. With practice and commitment, you may be able to transform that long-standing conflict into closeness.

PRACTICE

1. Practice recontextualizing the "problem" behavior in your relationship. What aspects of your partner's behavior have you been missing? What things have you been taking for granted? Notice the bigger picture, and let the parts that are truly most important to you become more central, more salient. Let the less important parts diminish.
2. Practice finding alternative meanings in your partner's behavior. How is his or her upbringing relevant? What is important to your partner? How might the problem behavior actually be something else, a reflection of lovable attributes (previously unnoticed)?
3. Embrace your partner as she is or he is. Enjoy what you have.

Engage in Your Life with Your Mate, Now!

In chapters 4 and 5, there were a lot of exercises designed to bring comfort and joy back into your partnership. Now is the time to revisit those activities, use the skills you have learned since, and enjoy the fact that you (hopefully) have less conflict, so that you can really be with each other in a more intimate, caring way.

Recall the various areas of your life that you can energize, and enjoy these activities together:
- Social and family time with other people
- Recreational and other fun activities together
- Sharing ideas and interests about whatever is important to you
- Sharing spiritual experiences and values
- Affectionate expression toward each other Sexual activities
- Sharing independent interests and supporting each other's autonomy
- Ordinary, day-to-day activities (even chores) around the house or yard, with kids, and so on

Mind the Gaps

Conflict is a result of many things, but in couples, it is mostly about a combination of misunderstanding, being judgmental, and bad habits. Each emotion, every thought, every reaction that your partner has that you do not understand (or misunderstand) becomes a painful gap in your relationship if you react negatively to that lack of understanding.

However, if you let go of judgments, you can be curious instead of only angry, interested instead of vindictive, and loving instead of attacking or running away. Instead of allowing negative habits to continue, notice what you don't know. Mind the gaps in your understanding of your partner and don't fill them up with negative assumptions, hopelessness, or despair. Ask instead of assuming, and show love and kindness instead of defensiveness or anger as your default mode. This is your partner, your love. You *can* form new habits that bring you closer and meet both of your needs for understanding, support, fun, and closeness.

Pay More Attention to What You Have Than to What You Don't Have

Life is finite, of course. If we truly recognize this, then we can ask the question, "How do I want to spend my day today?" with a renewed sense of importance. Do you want to spend your life noticing the blemishes only? Do you want to be most expert in criticizing your loved ones? Is that a desirable epitaph?

You do have a choice. You can notice mostly what is missing or contrary to your preferences, and feel disappointed, judgmental (assigning blame), and angry. Or you can more often notice what you have and endeavor to enjoy it fully. Of course, it is important to notice and self-validate when you don't have what you want or don't like what you have. There are effective times to work on making changes yourself, or together with your partner, to improve what you have. But, the vast majority of the time we have available to us is a mixture of more desirable and less desirable elements. What we pay attention to and how we pay attention will have a profound effect on our emotions and our satisfaction and, in turn, on our relationship. And, paradoxically, the more we accept and love what we actually have, the more it becomes what we want and love, and the easier it is to change the parts that are less desirable.

Remember, this is your partner, your love, your life. To be with him or her fully means not to be alone. Be with your partner. Most of the time, let go of your notions of how things should be and embrace what you have. Enjoy each other. Let go of your focus on differences or on loss (not having exactly what you want). Remember that the more you show interest and attention toward your partner, the more present your partner will be and the more interest and attention your partner will show you. There will be less conflict, more peace. The more you understand and validate, the more present she or he will be, and the more he or she will understand and validate you. The more you express yourself accurately and in a loving way, the more present and loving your partner will be. The more you appreciate and enjoy your partner, the more your partner will appreciate and enjoy you. There is tremendous peace in being with someone who loves you, as well as being with someone you love. Remember, this is your partner, your love, your life. Treat your partner as though your life depends on it. In fact, it does.

References

Addis, M.E., and C.R. Martell. 2004. *Overcoming Depression One Step at a Time.* Oakland, CA: New Harbinger Publications.

Baer, R.A. 2003. Mindfulness training as a clinical intervention: A conceptual and empirical review. *Clinical Psychology: Science and Practice* 10:125-143.

Barlow, D. H., ed. 1981. *Behavioral Assessment of Adult Disorders.* New York: Guilford Press.

Baumrind, D. 1971. Current Patterns of parental authority. *Developmental Psychology Monograph, Part 2,* 4:1-103.

Bishop, S.R., M. Lau, S. Shapiro, L. Carlson, N. Anderson, J. Carmody, Z. Segal, S. Abbey, M. Speca, D. Velting, and G. Devins. 2004. Mindfulness: A proposed operational definition. *Clinical Psychology: Science and Practice* 11:230-241.

Brown, G.W., and T.O. Harris. 1978. *Social Origins of Depression: A Study of Psychiatric Disorder in Women.* New York: Free Press.

Brown, K. W., and R. M. Ryan. 2003. The benefits of being present: Mindfulness and its role in psychological well-being. *Journal of Personality and Social Psychology* 84:822-848.

Campbell, L., and A.E. Fruzzetti. 2006. Cohesion as ersatz intimacy. Unpublished manuscript.

Cummings, E.M., and P.T. Davies. 1994. *Children and Marital Conflict.* New York: Guilford Press.

Fruzzetti, A. E. 1995. The closeness-distance family interaction coding system: A functional approach to coding couple and family interactions. Coding Manual, University of Nevada, Reno.

_____. 1996. Causes and consequences: Individual distress in the context of couple interactions. *Journal of*

Consulting and Clinical Psychology 64:1192-1201.

———. 1997. Dialectical behavior therapy skills for couples and families. Treatment Manual, University of Nevada, Reno.

———. 2002. Dialectical behavior therapy for borderline personality and related disorders. In *Cognitive Behavioral Approaches.* Vol. 2 of *Comprehensive Handbook of Psychotherapy,* ed. T. Patterson, 215-240. New York: Wiley.

Fruzzetti, A. E., and A. R. Fruzzetti. 2003. Borderline personality disorder. In *Treating Difficult Couples: Helping Clients with Coexisting Mental and Relationship Disorders,* ed. D. K. Snyder and M. A. Whisman, 235-260. New York: Guilford Press.

Fruzzetti, A. E., P. D. Hoffman, and D. Santisteban. Forthcoming. Dialectical behavior therapy adaptations for families. In *Adaptations of Dialectical Behavior Therapy,* ed. L. Dimeff, K.

Koerner, and M. Byars. New York: Guilford Press.

Fruzzetti, A. E., and K. M. Iverson. 2004. Mindfulness, acceptance, validation and "individual" psychopathology in couples. In *Mindfulness and Acceptance: Expanding the Cognitive-Behavioral Tradition,* ed. S. C. Hayes, V. M. Follette, and M. M. Linehan, 168-191. New York: Guilford Press.

_____. 2006. Intervening with couples and families to treat emotion dysregulation and psychopathology. In *Emotion Regulation in Families: Pathways to Dysfunction and Health,* ed. D.K. Snyder, J. Simpson, and J. Hughes. Washington, DC: American Psychological Association.

Fruzzetti, A.E., and N. S. Jacobson. 1990. Toward a behavioral conceptualization of adult intimacy: Implications for marital therapy. In *Emotions and the Family: For Better or for Worse,* ed. E. Blechman,

117-135. Hillsdale, NJ: Lawrence Erlbaum Associates.

Fruzzetti, A. E., and E. Mosco. 2006. Dialectical behavior therapy adapted for couples and families: A pilot group intervention for couples. Unpublished manuscript.

Fruzzetti, A.E., C. Shenk, and P.D. Hoffman. 2005. Family interaction and the development of borderline personality disorder: A transactional model. *Development and Psychopathology* 17:1007-1030.

Fruzzetti, A.E., C. Shenk, E. Mosco, and K. Lowry. 2003. Emotion regulation. In *Cognitive Behavior Therapy: Applying Empirically Supported Techniques in Your Practice,* ed. W.T. O'Donohue, J.E. Fisher, and S.C. Hayes, 152-159. New York: Wiley.

Fruzzetti, A.E., C. Shenk, E. Mosco, K. Lowry, and K.M. Iverson. 2006. Rating validating and invalidating behaviors in couples: Reliability and validity of new scales. Unpublished manuscript.

Gottman, J.M., and L.F. Katz. 1989. The effects of marital discord on young children's peer interaction and health. *Developmental Psychology* 25:373-381.

Greenberg, L.S., and S.M. Johnson. 1990. Emotional change processes in couples therapy. In *Emotions and the Family: For Better or for Worse,* ed. E. Blechman, 137-153. Hillsdale, NJ: Lawrence Erlbaum Associates.

Haynes, S.N. 1978. *Principles of Behavioral Assessment.* New York: Gardner Press.

Hoffman, P.D., A.E. Fruzzetti, E. Buteau, E. Neiditch, D. Penney, M. Bruce, F. Hellman, and E. Struening. 2005. Family connections: Effectiveness of a program for relatives of persons with borderline personality disorder. *Family Process* 44:217-225.

Hoffman, P.D., A.E. Fruzzetti, and C.R. Swenson. 1999. Dialectical behavior therapy: Family skills training. *Family Process* 38:399-414.

Iverson, K.M., and A.E. Fruzzetti. 2006. Validating and invalidating partner behaviors: Associations with distress and depression. Unpublished manuscript.

Jacobson, N.S., K.S. Dobson, A.E. Fruzzetti, K.B. Schmaling, and S. Salusky. 1991. Marital therapy as a treatment for depression. *Journal of Consulting and Clinical Psychology* 59:547-557.

Jacobson, N.S., K.S. Dobson, P. Truax, M.E. Addis, K. Koerner, J.K. Gollan, E. Gortner, and S. E. Prince. 1996. A component analysis of cognitive behavioral treatment for depression. *Journal of Consulting and Clinical Psychology* 64:295-304.

Jacobson, N.S., A.E. Fruzzetti, K. Dobson, M.A. Whisman, and H. Hops. 1993. Couple therapy as a treatment for depression: II. The effects of relationship quality and therapy on depressive relapse. *Journal of Consulting and Clinical Psychology* 61:516-519.

Jacobson, N.S., and G. Margolin. 1979. *Marital Therapy: Strategies Based on Social Learning and Behavior Exchange Principles.* New York: Brunner/Mazel.

Linehan, M.M. 1993a. *Cognitive-Behavioral Treatment of Borderline Personality Disorder.* New York: Guilford Press.

———. 1993b. *Skills Training Manual for Treating Borderline Personality Disorder.* New York: Guilford Press.

———. 1997. Validation and psychotherapy. In *Empathy and Psychotherapy: New Directions to Theory, Research, and Practice,* ed. A. Bohart and L.S. Greenberg, 353-392. Washington, DC: American Psychological Association.

Mandler, G. 1993. Thought, memory, and learning: Effects of emotional stress. In *Handbook of Stress: Theoretical and Clinical Aspects.* 2nd ed. Ed. L. Goldberger and S. Breznitz. New York: Free Press.

Nhât Hanh, T. 1975. *The Miracle of Mindfulness: A Manual on Meditation.* Boston: Beacon Press.

———. 1987. *Being Peace.* Berkeley, CA: Parallax Press.

Shenk, C., and A.E. Fruzzetti. 2006. The impact of validating and invalidating behavior on emotional arousal. Unpublished manuscript.

Weiss, R.L., and R.E. Heyman. 1997. A clinical-research overview of couple interactions. In *Clinical Handbook of Marriage and Couples Intervention,* ed. W.K. Halford and H. J. Markman, 13-42. New York: Wiley.

Whisman, M.A., and L.A. Uebelacker. 2003. Comorbidity of relationship distress and mental and physical health problems. In *Treating Difficult Couples: Helping Clients with Coexisting Mental and Relationship Disorders,* ed. D.K. Snyder and M.A. Whisman, 3-26. New York: Guilford Press.

Yerkes, R. M., and J. D. Dodson. 1908. The relation of strength of stimulus to rapidity of habit formation. *Journal of Comparative Neurology and Psychology* 18:459-482.

Alan E. Fruzzetti, Ph.D., is associate professor of psychology and director of the Dialectical Behavior Therapy and Research Program at the University of Nevada, Reno. He provides extensive training, supervision, and consultation for DBT treatment programs and DBT research in the United States and abroad.

Fruzzetti received his BA from Brown University and his Ph.D. from the University of Washington in Seattle. His research focuses on models of major psychopathology/severe behavior problems (e.g., borderline personality disorder, family violence, or chronic depression) in the context of couples and families, and the development and evaluation of effective treatments for these problems. In particular, he focuses on the further development, evaluation, and training of dialectical behavior therapy (DBT) with individuals, couples and families for chronic or severe individual and/or family distress.

Fruzzetti is also research director and member of the board of directors of the National Educational Alliance for Borderline Personality Disorder and a codeveloper of the Family Connections Program. He has provided extensive DBT training in the United States, Europe, and Australia. He has authored or coauthored dozens of scholarly articles and book chapters on this and related topics.

Foreword writer **Marsha M. Linehan, Ph.D.,** is professor of psychology and director of the Behavioral Research and Therapy Clinics (BRTC) at the University of Washington in Seattle, WA. She is author of *Cognitive Behavioral Treatment of Borderline Personality Disorder* and *Skills Training Manual for Treating Borderline Personality Disorder.*

www.ingramcontent.com/pod-product-compliance
Lightning Source LLC
Chambersburg PA
CBHW050329230426
43663CB00010B/1792